C000130530

THE COMPLETE GUIDE TO COCKAPOO DOGS

David Anderson

Special thanks to Erin Hotovy
for her work on this project

LP Media Inc. Publishing

Text copyright © 2018 by LP Media Inc.

All rights reserved.

www.lpmedia.org

Publication Data

Anderson, David.

The Complete Guide to Cockapoo Dogs / David Anderson. ---- First edition.

Summary: "Successfully raising a Cockapoo dog from puppy to old age" --- Provided by publisher.

ISBN: 978-1792775321

[1. Cockapoo --- Non-Fiction] I. Title.

Design by Sorin Radulescu

First paperback edition, 2018

TABLE OF CONTENTS

CHAPTER 1
Introduction to Cockapoos

"Cockapoos are people pleasers; they love nothing more than to make the people around them happy! They are a happy go lucky breed that is perfectly content snuggling on the couch with you, or taking a trek through the woods: they just go with the flow. They are also incredibly intelligent and there is no limit to the things that they can be taught!"

Jamie

Cute Cockapoos

Bringing a new dog into your life is an exciting occasion, especially if the dog is a Cockapoo! This breed is cute, cuddly, and so much fun to have as a companion. However, a new dog is a lot of work. Before you even get the chance to pick out your dog, you'll need to think about things like breeders, training, and supplies. Don't worry—this book will guide you through everything you need to know about owning a Cockapoo! We'll cover it all, from food and exercise to grooming and vet care. By the end, you'll be more than ready to open your home to a new best friend.

What is a Cockapoo?

The Cockapoo is not a single dog breed—instead, it's a cross between a Poodle and a Cocker Spaniel. On their own, both breeds are fine dogs, but together, they create a super-hybrid that you'll be sure to love. Like many Poodle crossbreeds, this breed has a curly, fluffy coat and can vary in size, depending on breeding.

A Cockapoo is often designated as a "designer dog". This means that there is no purebred standard for them. Instead, two breeds are crossed to take desirable traits from one breed and infuse it within another. Designer breeds have become increasingly popular in recent decades, and there are tons of different hybrids out there for potential dog owners to choose. But this varied lineage does not mean that designer dogs are mutts—they are carefully bred and adored by organizations dedicated to the hybrids.

Photo Courtesy of Jaci Ingham

Understanding the Cockapoo's Lineage

You'll find that a Cockapoo has the very best qualities of the Poodle and Cocker Spaniel. This breed has a curly coat with big, floppy ears. They have a lot of energy but are also intelligent and easy to train. To understand this cross breed, it helps to understand the common traits attributed to the Poodle and Cocker Spaniel as individual breeds.

Poodles are commonly used in crossbreeding designer dogs, and for good reason. Perhaps the most obvious desirable trait is their curly coat. A Poodle crossbreed's fur tends to mix textures with whatever breed it is crossed with. A straight-haired breed will yield wavy-haired offspring when crossed with a Poodle. Also, Poodles are bred to be different sizes, leading to some variation and choice when it comes to the Cockapoo. Standard Poodles can grow to be rather large, so the Miniature and Toy Poodle were created. When you see breeders advertise smaller-than-average Cockapoos, it's likely that the Cocker Spaniel is bred with one of these smaller types of Poodles.

While the Poodle is often stereotyped as being pompous and prissy, this is not the case with the breed. Poodles are one of the more intelligent dog breeds, meaning that training is easy with them. They are sensitive dogs, so they are able to take in a lot of information from their surroundings. This is a good thing when it comes time to train your dog, as a sensitive dog cares about the nonverbal cues their owner presents. A sensitive dog generally wants to please their owner, so they are able to better understand what you want and adjust their behavior accordingly.

Poodles also have a ton of energy and require lots of play and exercise. As with any intelligent breed, mental stimulation is just as important as physical exercise. This dog can get along well in a small home or apartment as long as the owner commits a few hours to exercise and play each day.

The Cocker Spaniel is much smaller than the standard Poodle and rarely grows to be larger than thirty pounds. This dog's coat is very thick with a slightly wavy texture. This is one of those breeds where frequent grooming is non-negotiable; without regular brushing and trimming, the coat will turn into a matted mess. This breed also has adorable floppy ears, which are prone to infection, especially if moisture is trapped underneath.

Cocker Spaniels are friendly dogs, and they are very much owner-oriented. They want to spend as much time as possible with their favorite people and dislike being left alone. They are moderately stranger-, kid-, and dog-friendly, though they are highly sensitive and may initially distrust others until they have the time to sniff them out. They may also bark at the sound of a doorbell, as they will want to protect their owner from whatever unknown danger is out there. With this breed, socialization is key because they need to learn how to get along with a variety of people and animals.

As is the case with other small breeds, Cocker Spaniels don't require as much exercise as larger dogs. They are playful and energetic, but not to the point where they are unmanageable. This dog is satisfied with a nice walk at the end of the day, with lots of cuddles and attention in between.

You'll find that the Cockapoo is really the happy medium between these two dog breeds. They're full of energy, but not constantly bouncing off the walls. They have a coat that requires grooming, but don't shed a lot of fur. They are cuddly and very friendly towards others. It's no surprise that this crossbreed has been popular for so many years.

Photo Courtesy of
Fiona Reid

Cockapoo History

Photo Courtesy of Lesley Gibbs

While Poodle crossbreeds have been extremely popular in recent years, the Cockapoo has been around longer than you'd think! This breed dates back nearly sixty years ago. It's not certain if the first Poodle/Cocker Spaniel was purposeful, but the breeder liked the result they got and it took off from there. Since then, breeders have continued to perfect this cross to produce the most desirable traits in this dog.

In 1999, the Cockapoo Club of America was created to promote a breed standard. Because this is not a pure breed that dates back to an era where dogs were workers, there were no official standards to aim for. Appearance and dispositional traits were mainly up to the individual, as there was no official kennel club designation to provide breeders with these standards and rules. This club prefers breeders to use Cockapoos in their crosses, instead of creating a first-generation Poodle/Cocker Spaniel pup, in order to maintain some consistency in the breed.

On the other hand, the American Cockapoo Club, founded in 2004, discourages members from crossing multi-generational Cockapoos with one another and promotes the breeding of Poodles and Cocker Spaniels. As you can see, there's more than one way to breed a Cockapoo! While both groups have differences in bringing about the perfect Cockapoo, both stress the importance of skilled and responsible breeding in order to keep the breed intact.

With these organizations and standards, breeders are able to produce litters of Cockapoos with similar characteristics. That way, when you buy a Cockapoo from a breeder, you have a good idea of what you're getting. Breed standards do not only affect the appearance of the dog, but also the behavioral characteristics.

Physical Characteristics

The standard Cockapoo is not a small dog. Often referred to as a "Maxi Cockapoo", these dogs are more than nineteen pounds and at least fifteen inches tall. This breed also has a single coat that can come in a range of textures. The curly or wavy coat is the most common, but straight-coated Cockapoos also exist. Generally, these dogs have a full, fluffy coat that does not require shaving to keep under control. However, when the fur occludes the eyes, a trim is needed to keep the dog looking neat and clean.

As is the case with many crossbreeds, there is a wide variety in coat colors, with some more common than others. Black, white, cream, brown, buff, and red are all coat colors seen in Cockapoos. Of course, some dogs have two or three of these colors in their coat. The variation is caused by the parents' coat colors, so if you're interested in buying a dog with a particular coat color, talk to your breeder about the possibilities of their puppies showing those traits.

This breed also comes in a variety of sizes. The standard Cockapoo is the largest and is over nineteen pounds. The next smallest is the miniature Cockapoo at thirteen and eighteen pounds and between eleven and fourteen inches tall. Smaller yet is the toy Cockapoo, which is less than twelve pounds and ten inches tall. And, if that isn't small enough for you, the teacup toy Cockapoo is also about ten inches tall but weighs under six pounds.

Photo Courtesy of Misty Reece

"Hypoallergenic Dogs"

One of the major reasons these dogs are so popular is because they are often referred to as "hypoallergenic." The Cockapoo definitely sheds less than a Cocker Spaniel and might create less of an allergic response in humans, but no dog is fully hypoallergenic.

Generally, the curlier the coat, the less likely the dog is to shed. When a dog doesn't shed excessively, that means that less of their dander spreads around your home. Since dander is often the thing that causes people to feel sneezy around pets, a dog with less of this is typically easier on the sinuses. For someone with less severe allergies, a dog with a curlier coat may be enough to keep one's allergies at bay entirely.

But if the owner has a moderate to severe dog allergy, they might not get away with having a Poodle crossbreed in their home. It's also possible to be allergic to a dog's saliva. And you may find that you're more allergic to some dogs but not others even within the same litter. So if you have a dog allergy, it may not be enough to buy a Poodle crossbreed. Their curly coat may prevent some issues and may keep your home cleaner than if you had a Cocker Spaniel, but there is no completely hypoallergenic dog.

Behavioral Characteristics

Though many choose their future dog based on appearance alone, temperament is important when selecting the right dog for your household. Luckily, this breed is easy-going and has a lot to offer for a variety of households. Cockapoos are generally friendly with just about anyone they come into contact with. They are companion dogs that want to make their owners happy and to be at their side as much as possible. Unfortunately, that means that these dogs may be prone to separation anxiety if left alone for too long.

Cockapoos are smart dogs that benefit from obedience training. They enjoy learning new skills and tricks. These dogs have plenty of playful energy, but not to the degree that a dog like a Poodle has. They are manageable for any owner who can provide them with a moderate amount of exercise.

Photo Courtesy of
Julie Bootle

Is a Cockapoo Right for Me?

Before you bring a Cockapoo into your household, it's important to have a thorough and honest look at your ability and willingness to provide everything a Cockapoo, or any dog, needs. The amount of attention, physical energy, and time varies from breed to breed, so it's a good idea to make sure you and your home are fit for a Cockapoo before bringing one home.

First, examine your housing situation. If you live in an apartment or small house, it might not be enough room for a standard Cockapoo. However, you can always consider buying one of the smaller variations, as they do not require as much room to roam. A backyard with a fence is also an added bonus for a dog, as it allows them more room to run and play in a safe environment. A little extra space can make a huge difference in your dog's overall happiness when it comes to their ability to burn energy. But, unlike many other breeds, a smaller home is not a deal breaker with this dog.

Next, think about your time commitments. These are companion animals and will want to be around you as much as possible. So, if you work a job where you're never home, you might want to consider a different pet that doesn't form as strong of a connection to you. It varies from dog to dog, but Cockapoos are susceptible to separation anxiety if they feel neglected. You'll want to have plenty of quality time to spend with your pup, especially in the early days.

This dog has moderate exercise requirements, so a few quick walks each day and some extra playtime is sufficient. Your dog will need this exercise no matter the weather, so you'll have to commit to walking for twenty minutes or more at a time. The smaller variations require a bit less exercise, if that makes a difference for you and your lifestyle.

Finally, you'll have to do some training with this dog. Cockapoos are generally pretty friendly, but their Cocker Spaniel genes might make them a little extra cautious. For this reason, it's important to get your puppy socialized and trained to behave around other animals, children, and strangers. This breed does best with some obedience training and regular practice. Training can be fun, but it can also be frustrating at times. Cockapoos are sensitive animals and respond best to positive training methods. Are you someone who can dedicate time to training and do so in an upbeat method? If so, you'll have no problem training this dog.

If you can read through this quick list of prerequisites for Cockapoo ownership and honestly say that you can fulfill each item, then it's time to start preparing for your new dog! If not, you may find that it's best to wait until you're at a stage in your life where you're better prepared to own a Cockapoo. Owning a Cockapoo is a lot of work, and everyone involved will be so much happier if you're fully prepared for the responsibility. But the great thing about Cockapoos is that they are generally easy to take care of.

Cockapoos make great pets for people of all ages and backgrounds. If you show them love and kindness, they will return the favor. When it comes to their appearance, there is so much variation that you have options when it comes to picking out the cutest. And their bubbly personalities will ensure that you immediately fall in love with them. There's still a lot of work to do before bringing home your new best friend, but by the time you reach the end of the book, you'll hopefully feel fully prepared for your new Cockapoo!

CHAPTER 2
Choosing Your Cockapoo

Now that you've settled that this is the right breed for you, it's time to figure out how to find the right dog. When choosing a new companion, there's more to it than just going to a pet store and picking out the cutest dog. You'll need to do some research and think about what's important to you when it comes to getting a new dog.

Buying vs. Adopting

Photo Courtesy of Samantha Harwood

The first choice to make is whether you want to buy or adopt your new dog. This decision should be made on what is best for you and your home. People will inevitably try to persuade you to go one route or the other; in the end, you know what's best for you.

There are lots of benefits to purchasing a dog from a good breeder. First, you'll have a good idea of what your future dog is going to look and act like because breeding is a science. Before the puppies are even born, the breeder will be able to tell you the traits of their pups because they've spent time with the parents and have gotten to know previous litters. While an inexperienced breeder may end up with sickly dogs with behavioral issues, a good breeder knows what traits are important in a Cockapoo.

Some owners like to start from scratch when it comes to raising their new dog. If you're the only influence on the dog from an early age, you'll have control over how the dog is brought up. If you start with a new puppy, you'll make the rules from Day One. If you adopt a dog that's had a previous owner, it's hard to know what the dog has learned from that person. Many times, the dog has no trouble adjusting to life with a new owner, but you may find that the dog has learned bad habits that take some work to undo.

*Photo Courtesy of
Susie Thomas*

On the other hand, there are also many benefits to adoption. Of course, perhaps the best aspect about adopting is knowing that you're giving a dog a much needed forever home. Many adoption advocates claim that a rescue dog is more appreciative of their owner. Whether or not this is true, it's undeniable how good it feels to give a dog a second chance at life.

Also, if you aren't interested in spending a thousand dollars or more on a Cockapoo puppy, adoption is much more affordable. Shelters generally charge a small fee, but this also includes veterinary services such as vaccination and spay/neuter surgeries. This allows you to save a little money to be spent on spoiling your pup with the best treats and toys!

Adoption is also beneficial if you're apprehensive about training a new puppy. Some adopted dogs will need a refresher course on basic training if they didn't come from a good home, but many surrendered Cockapoos come from good homes that fell into unfortunate circumstances. It's possible to get an adult Cockapoo that is potty-trained and knows some basic commands. Training a puppy is hard work and is very time consuming, so it can be nice to have a little help from a previous owner. Puppies are cute, but they're rambunctious and require a ton of care. You may find that a mellower adult Cockapoo is exactly what you need.

19

Photo Courtesy of Greta Sheridan

If you decide you want to buy a puppy, it's important to find the right breeder. Because Cockapoos are considered to be a designer dog, this is especially important. Inexperienced breeders often jump in on trends because it's an easy way to make extra money. Unfortunately, when people breed dogs without the right expertise, it leads to inconsistencies with the standard. It can result in dogs with genetic defects and bad behavioral traits. Essentially, you'll be sold an inferior product at a high price.

How to Find a Good Breeder

A good breeder knows exactly what they're doing and has the experience to back it up. These people breed dogs for the love of the breed, not just for money. They work with the best stock and produce puppies that win competitions. But you need to know how to identify a good breeder.

If you've come to love the Cockapoo, there's a good chance that you know someone else who has one. If the owner is happy with their dog, absolutely ask them who their breeder was. Breeders love to get referrals from satisfied customers. If you don't know anyone with a Cockapoo, you'll have to do a little extra research on your own.

Start out with a list of Cockapoo breeders in your area. If they have a website or social media page, look at the image they present. However, there's only so much you can tell about a breeder from their web presence. To know more, you'll have to ask questions and look at their facilities.

A good breeder will welcome any and all questions you can think of. They are passionate about Cockapoos and want to be able to share their knowledge with you. After all, they worked hard and spent a lot of time educating themselves on the breed.

During this information-gathering process, you should ask the breeder about health clearances. These are certificates that a breeder should provide to you to guarantee that your puppy will not experience genetic illnesses later in life. The parents of your new puppy should be in excellent health, as certified by a veterinarian. A less-reputable breeder may not have this kind of assurance

*Photo Courtesy of
Pat Johnson*

Photo Courtesy of
Judith Hathaway

available or may even try to hide that information. You may also want to ask for references of satisfied owners of the pups. Some breeders also require you to take the puppy to a veterinarian within the first few months after you bring your dog home, just to ensure that the buyer is happy with their dog's health. This protects the breeder if the buyer later decides they don't want the dog and they try to make excuses for a return. This practice is good for both the breeder and the new owner to ensure that the new puppy is as healthy as can be.

If possible, try to visit the breeder's home. The area where the puppies are kept should be clean and free of animal waste. They should have enough room to move around and spend time with their siblings, not locked in a tiny cage. If a breeder doesn't allow you to come to their home or seems secretive about how the puppies are looked after, you should stay away.

Finally, ask about certifications. A breeder should be eager to tell you about the Cockapoo associations they belong to or the different dog clubs they're a part of. Make sure they really care about the breed and aren't just trying to make a buck off of a fad.

Choosing Your Cockapoo

Once you've found the right breeder, it's time to choose the dog. It may be tempting to choose your new puppy based on a picture alone, but if you really want the pick of the litter, an in-person visit can help you find the right dog.

While a good breeder will do their best to make sure the puppies have the best temperament possible, you'll still notice subtle variation within a litter. Just like with human siblings, each puppy has their own unique personality. If you get the opportunity to pick from the entire litter, spend a little time playing with the puppies and observe how they respond to both people and the other dogs. Then, choose a dog that falls somewhere in the middle of the personality spectrum.

For example, you may notice that some puppies are very rambunctious, while others are submissive and shy. Neither extreme is best, so you want the puppy that is playful but also capable of being calm and sweet. An overly dominant puppy may turn into a stubborn dog, and a shy pup might develop anxiety or phobias. Of course, many behaviors are learned later on, but finding a pup that falls somewhere in a happy medium of personality traits might help you on your way to puppy parenthood. Also, don't underestimate your first instinct. If you find yourself bonding with a particular dog, that might be the one for you.

If a Cockapoo is your dream dog because you have allergies, it's especially important that you check the puppies out in person. You'll want to make sure you feel okay after spending some time around the dogs. You may even want to allow the puppies to give you kisses, just to make sure their saliva doesn't cause an allergic reaction either. Never assume a dog will not give you an allergic response just because it's advertised as hypoallergenic. Everybody is different, and what works for other people may not work for you.

Adoption Tips

If you decide that you'd rather go with the adoption route, there are a few ways to make sure you end up with the perfect Cockapoo. Local shelters can be hit-or-miss when it comes to having the right breed. This is where adoption and rescue websites come in handy. Websites like PetFinder.com allow you to search for specific breeds in your area. If you select a wider search radius, you can find all the Cockapoos within whatever distance you're willing to drive to adopt a dog. Or you can do your own search for Cockapoo rescues. These are organizations that collect Cockapoos from shelters and re-home them to good owners.

Don't assume that adopting a dog is as simple as paying a fee and picking up your new Cockapoo. Because these dogs were once surrendered, the volunteers who run these shelters are very particular about the homes they go to next. Too much change can be hard on a dog, so they want their next home to be their last home for the rest of their life. Especially with Cockapoo rescues, you can expect a detailed application form and even home visit. They'll want to know who lives in your home and if you have any other pets. They'll want to know where you live, what kind of experience you have with dogs, and if you have a backyard fence without any gaps for a dog to squeeze through.

If your web search brings up a dog, don't feel obligated to adopt it. Perhaps you had your heart set on an adult dog and the one in the shelter is a puppy. Or maybe it's documented to be bad with children and you have kids at home. It can be hard to wait for the perfect dog to appear in a shelter near you, but it's best not to force a dog into a situation that isn't right for you. You'll only end up with problems and will have to return the dog to the shelter. It may take a little time to find the right Cockapoo to adopt, but it will absolutely be worth it when you're able to bring your dog to their new forever home.

Once you decide you want a Cockapoo in your home, it's hard not to rush things and buy the first dog that's available. Take your time and explore all of your options. Not only does this allow you to get the best pup for you, but you'll have time to figure out what you need to make your future dog's life as perfect as possible. Support good breeders who use ethical practices instead of funding backyard breeding operations. Also, ask as many questions as you can think up! A breeder is a great source of knowledge for all things Cockapoo. Learn as much as you can from them so your dog's transition into your home is a smooth one.

Photo Courtesy of Dondra Blackwell

CHAPTER 3
Preparing Your Home for Your Cockapoo

"I recommend to families, that their home should be child proof. As with any puppy, there an adjustment period; they need to acclimate to the new families' routine and smells."

Luann Woodard
Cockapoo Cottage

While you're in the process of finding the right breeder or shelter, it's the ideal time to start preparing your home for your new Cockapoo. Bringing a new dog into your home without any preparation is a good way to inflict unnecessary stress upon you and your new pup. Because you want your new dog's life with you to start out smoothly, you'll want to have everything in order before the big day. This means you'll need to get everyone in your household prepared for dog ownership, prepare spaces for the pup, and remove any hidden dangers in your home.

Photo Courtesy of Vikki Whitworth

Adjusting Pets and Children

In time, your dog will learn how to socialize with people and other animals so that they can get along with everybody. Until then, it's necessary to teach the other people (and pets) in your household how to behave around a new puppy.

If this is your first dog and you have children, this is going to be a very exciting time for everyone. But unless your child has lots of experience with animals, they might not know how to behave around a dog. It's vital to teach kids how to act around dogs, because a dog will have little control over their instincts. They may be sweet as can be, but when faced with a perceived danger, they will act like an animal.

The Cockapoo is a very sensitive dog that tends to be friendly around kids, but still has its limits. Lots of loud noises may overstimulate or frighten this breed, especially if the dog has yet to get used to strange sounds. When dogs are scared, they usually try to remove themselves from the situation first. If this isn't possible, they might become aggressive.

For example, let's say your new Cockapoo is being poked and prodded in uncomfortable places by excited kids. Their first reaction may be to run away from the problem. But kids are persistent and may corner the pup and continue their rough petting. A frightened dog will growl and bare its teeth, but this may also go unnoticed by a young child who doesn't understand a dog's special language (or think it's funny or part of a game). Finally, the dog will snap—their final warning that they're stressed and need some space. Unfortunately, this can be very frightening and dangerous to a child and could create more issues for your household.

One way to prevent this type of situation from occurring is to teach your children your dog's warning signs. If they see their dog cowering away from them, tell them that the dog needs space, like a timeout. This way, both your dog and your children can take a moment to chill out.

Even the gentlest dog will not enjoy being poked and prodded with little fingers. It's not unheard of for a curious child to go poking around the eyes or ears, which can be very sensitive for a dog. The little wagging tail of your Cockapoo is irresistible, but your dog will not like being grabbed by it. Teach kids how to "pet nicely" by running a flat palm from the back of the neck to the base of the tail. This is a good way for young kids to bond with their new pet without the risk of getting bitten.

If you have pets, you'll want them to be acquainted with your Cockapoo early on. If your breeder allows you to take the pup away from their premises to meet your pets, that will help you out a lot in the long run. If you're adopting, the shelter or rescue will likely allow you (and encourage you) to take the Cockapoo home to check things out.

This process may take several steps before you're at the point where you're comfortable having your pets together. Dogs don't like to be forced into interacting with strange animals, and their resistance can set you back if things don't go well in the first meeting.

For your first meeting, choose neutral ground. Dogs are notoriously territorial, and even the best-behaved pup may act aggressively around a strange dog if they feel like their space is threatened. Your old dog may not get along with another dog if it's in his home. A park or a friend's backyard is a great place to set up this meeting, as neither dog will feel like they 'own' the space. You may even ask your breeder if it's okay to bring your dog to their home, as there will likely be a lot of room to roam around.

Now, it's time to call in reinforcements. Because it can be difficult to juggle two dogs, ask a friend or family member to help you with the introduction stage. Put each dog on a secure leash to prevent an incident from happening. Slowly approach your friend with the other dog and let the two pups sniff each other out. Remain calm and casual, and don't force the dogs to interact if they're not interested in it. Also, give the dogs plenty of time to sniff. There's a lot of information that can be gained from sniffing a behind, so allow them to make their full introductions in the manner that dogs usually do.

If this meeting goes without an issue, then you're on your way to making both dogs feel comfortable together. If not, give the dogs plenty of space and try again another time.

If your dogs passed the first step, it's time to reunite them in your house. You might even want to take another baby step and let the dogs check each other out in the backyard before moving to inside the home. Repeat the process with the dogs on separate leashes and give them the chance to get comfortable around the house. If everything goes well, you may even decide to let them play around a little. Be cautious and make sure that play doesn't turn into fighting. However, you may notice that your older dog may want to put the puppy in his place as the beta dog in the relationship.

If things don't go so well, that doesn't mean all hope is lost for a peaceful household! It may take some time for your dogs to feel comfortable around each other. Let your dogs have a little time and space apart and try again later. It can be frustrating when progress seems slow, but it's best to be patient so that everyone is happy and comfortable.

*Photo Courtesy of
Karen Oakley*

Household Dangers

Photo Courtesy of Susie Thomas

Once everything is squared away with your children and other pets, it's time to make sure your house is ready for your new dog. If this is your only dog, you may not realize that there are hidden dangers around your house for a canine. Spend a little time examining your home for things that could be dangerous for a new puppy. Think of it as "baby-proofing" your house for your new arrival.

Especially when dealing with puppies, just assume that everything your dog can reach will get chewed on. You may be in the habit of kicking your shoes off at the front door and leaving them there, but a dog will wait until you're not around and chew them to shreds. Start getting into the habit of picking up items that are within reach for a dog. Shoes, cords, and remote controls on coffee tables are all frequently-chewed items. These things can pose a risk for electric shock or choking if your puppy is a big chewer. Smaller items, like socks and underwear, can go missing and require a vet's help to retrieve them.

You'd be surprised at how crafty a Cockapoo can be. Their intelligence allows them to figure out how to get into the things they want. If cleaning supplies are in plain sight or even on top of the counter, it's feasible for a dog to get a hold of a bottle and ingest dangerous chemicals. Or if you have cleaning chemicals in your toilet bowl, a Cockapoo might want to have a little drink. Make sure that there's no way for your dog to access cleaning supplies, because a curious dog will want to try everything.

It's great to have a fenced-in backyard because you can let your dog spend time in the fresh air without constant supervision, but if you're not careful, your dog can become very sick from innocuous-looking plants. If you have a lot of landscaping in your yard, take a close look at what's planted out there. There are tons of common plants that can make your dog very sick if they decide to munch on one. Ivy, lilies, and hostas are common outdoor plants that are toxic to dogs. If a small Cockapoo eats one of these, it won't take much to make them sick. If you're concerned about growing any dangerous plants in your yard, do a search for plants that are toxic to dogs. Many websites contain lists and pictures to help you identify plants that are not safe for dogs to eat. Not all dogs will want to take a big bite out of your decorative plants, but it's good to be aware of some of these hidden dangers.

Also, do a sweep through your garage and garden shed before bringing your dog home. While they might not have a lot of access to these areas, in the event they do, you don't want certain items to be at snout-level. Basically, anything you wouldn't want a child to eat you will want to move out of reach for your dog. This includes pesticides, fertilizers, or rodent killers. The sticky mousetrap you put in the corner of the garage years ago and forgot about will easily be found by your dog. If you've gotten accustomed to life without a curious dog that is determined to get into everything, it's easy to overlook things that have never been a problem in the past. Take caution in the products you use around your yard and home, especially if your Cockapoo is going to be allowed to roam around the backyard alone on a frequent basis.

Preparing Spaces for Your Cockapoo

This is also the time to begin thinking about the spaces in your home that you're allowing access to. If you're planning on keeping your Cockapoo outside often, seriously consider where you spend the bulk of your time. Cockapoos need to spend a lot of time around their people. If you plan on keeping your dog outside all the time while you're inside, your dog will become very lonely. You don't necessarily need to let your dog sleep in your bed, but allowing your dog to spend time with you indoors is vital to your Cockapoo's happiness. This is not a breed that can be left outside all day long.

However, a puppy can wreak havoc in a house if left unchecked. Don't feel as though you need to let your Cockapoo have the run of the house. Close any doors that you don't want your dog venturing through and use gates to keep them from stumbling downstairs or wandering through hallways that are off-limits. You want your dog to have plenty of room to roam, but it's good to give your puppy boundaries early on.

One way to make your dog feel comfortable in your home is to give them some personal space. Designate a part of the house to keep your dog's bed or crate. The corner of the kitchen or living room is a good choice because it allows your social dog to be part of the family while also having some private room to relax.

Once you set up this space with comfortable blankets and toys, leave them alone. This teaches them that if they feel scared or uncomfortable,

31

Photo Courtesy of
Emma Balsom

they can go to that spot for a little "time out". When your Cockapoo is ready to be around people, they'll let you know! Giving your dog their own space allows them to clearly tell you when they're stressed or annoyed. It can be tempting to bother them, but it's important to leave them be when they retreat to their bed or crate.

For example, you might have a dog that hates having their toenails cut. They may sit or wiggle around for the first few toenails, but at a certain point, they have reached their threshold of tolerance and need to escape before they act out. If they jump up and curl up in a ball on their bed, it can be tempting to pin them down and finish the job. You must resist this urge! If you violate their space, then they no longer have a safe spot to chill out. You can always wait until later to finish the job—let them have their moment and prevent them from acting out when they get agitated.

If you plan on letting your dog spend time outside without supervision, you may want to set up a comfy spot for them in the backyard as well. When the weather is nice, a lot of owners let their dog chill out in the fresh air for a few hours while they're away. Unfortunately, a change in weather can be unexpected. Make sure you have a spot in your yard that provides plenty of shade on hot, sunny days. If you don't have a lot of trees or shrubs for your dog to rest under, consider getting an awning or umbrella for your deck. This will also provide protection from the rain and snow.

A fence is vital if you want to let your Cockapoo run around in the safety of your own backyard while unsupervised. A Cockapoo owner will require different things when it comes to a fence, depending on the type of Cockapoo you have. If you have one of the smaller variations, you need to be very careful about making sure they can't squeeze out of any gaps. It doesn't take a lot of digging for a little Cockapoo to make a break for it. Or, if you have a short fence, you'd be surprised at how springy your standard Cockapoo is if they see a squirrel on the other side of the street. If you're installing a fence for your new Cockapoo, you might also want to consider choosing something that doesn't allow visibility through the fence. A chain-link fence may be a more affordable option, but consider how much your dog will want to bark at people in neighboring houses.

After teaching kids how to behave around a new dog, teaching dogs how to behave around the new Cockapoo, and doing a quick sweep of your home, you'll feel more prepared to bring the new puppy to their new home. Cockapoos are sensitive and can pick up on their owner's stress levels, so if you want your new puppy to feel calm, you need to feel calm too. Knowing that your dog will be safe in your home will go a long way to making you feel at ease with a new Cockapoo in the family.

Photo Courtesy of Maria McNamara

CHAPTER 4
Bringing Your Cockapoo Home

"The Cockapoo is an excellent breed for in-town living. They are not a 'high-energy' dog but still require a couple walks outside a day or a fenced backyard to play in."

Alisa Foerderer
Foerderer Horses and Cock-a-poos

The preparation is not over yet! You may be in the process of figuring out when you're going to bring your new Cockapoo home, but there's still some more work to do to ensure the transition into your home is as smooth as possible. It might seem excessive to go through all of these measures just for a dog, but you'll find that the preparation is absolutely worth it.

This chapter will walk you through a few important things to consider in the early days of having your new Cockapoo at home. It will discuss things you need to arrange early on, plus a few items you should have on hand. Finally, we'll break down the average costs of owning a Cockapoo in the first year of its life so that there are no surprises for you down the road.

Dogs are perceptive creatures, and the Cockapoo is even more so than other breeds. They have a way of noticing how you feel by paying attention to your non-verbal cues. They can tell when you're happy and they know when you're upset. Sometimes, dogs look to their people to tell them how they should feel. If you're happy and excited, then your dog will mirror that and respond similarly. If you're stressed out and overwhelmed, your dog may take that as a cue to panic because something is obviously wrong. They may not understand that their arrival is the cause of the stress, but they're still likely to feel some of that anxiety. So, the less stress you feel about your new arrival, the smoother things will go for everyone in the household.

Photo Courtesy of
Jenna Galpin

The First Night Home

The first night at home will likely be pretty rough. Your dog will be in a completely new setting without their mother or siblings. They will cry a lot and want you to soothe them. Also, if your Cockapoo is a puppy, they will also need to go to the bathroom frequently. If you're not used to getting up multiple times in the middle of the night, this will be a big change for you.

If you're crate training (which you should seriously consider), you may want to put the crate in a place close to where you sleep. That way, your dog will know that you are near and haven't abandoned them, and you can hear when they cry because they need to go to the bathroom or need to be comforted. Especially in the early days, prepare for your sleep to be interrupted by your dog. As your dog becomes more comfortable in your home, you can move their crate or bed further away. Some owners like to sleep with their dog in their bed. While this is completely up to personal preference, just remember that there will be times where you don't want your Cockapoo hogging your bed. You can push them off, but they might not understand why they can sleep there sometimes but not at other times.

If you want to prevent accidents during the night, prepare to get up every few hours to walk your dog outside. A puppy cannot hold their potty for more than an hour or two, so unless you want to clean up a mess in the morning, you'll have to get out of bed and go outside when they cry.

Nighttime is a good opportunity to close all the other doors in your house and set up gates. If you leave your home open to your dog, you may change your mind about that decision when you wake up the next morning. If you're not awake to supervise your dog's movements, you may discover that they like to explore and soothe themselves by chewing on your furniture. An unsupervised dog can get into a lot of trouble very quickly, so minimize risk by keeping the majority of your home off-limits at bedtime.

Your first night might be very stressful for your new dog, and this stress may not fully dissipate for a week or two. Your dog is learning how to live life with a new human in a new place without their family members surrounding them. Their cries at nighttime the first few days are no indication of their overall happiness with you—they're just getting used to their new home. Before long, they'll be sleeping through the night.

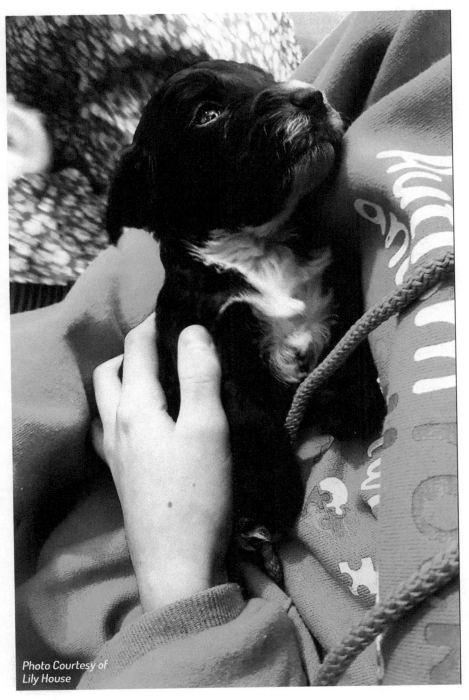

Photo Courtesy of
Lily House

How to Find a Vet

During the first week or two, it's important to decide where you are going to take your Cockapoo for their veterinary care. If you live in a city where there are plenty of choices, it can be hard to decide. Friends, breeders, rescue volunteers, and trainers are all good sources for referrals. Also, prices and services will vary from office to office, so you may need to do some "shopping" to find one that fits your needs. For example, the small clinic closest to your home may be a fine place for check-ups and general care, but they may not have a laboratory or surgical facilities. This means that if your dog needs advanced care, they would have to go to a different clinic. Either option is valid, but it's a good idea to know the full range of services before you settle on a vet.

If your regular vet does not have emergency services, it's recommended to find your closest emergency vet clinic and write down their contact information. You never know when something bad might happen to your Cockapoo, and you don't want to wait for an emergency to start your research. Keep the phone number and address stored in your cell phone so you can quickly contact and locate them if an accident happens.

Photo Courtesy of Natalie McGuigan

Photo Courtesy of Katherine Hanke

Puppy Training

Also, within the first month or two of dog ownership, you'll want to find a puppy training class for your new Cockapoo. All dogs should go through some training course, but this is especially important for smart breeds like the Cockapoo. There are many benefits to continuous training, which will be covered in detail in later chapters.

A puppy training course is a good way to learn how to train a new dog, especially if you don't have a lot of experience with training. Every dog is different, and if you've trained a dog in the past, you might find that your Cockapoo has a different personality with a different learning style. A trainer-led session is great for picking up tips and tricks for turning your Cockapoo puppy into an obedient adult.

These classes will focus on the very basics of obedience. You'll likely practice walking your dog on a leash without pulling and simple commands like "sit" and "down". Your puppy is still learning on how to live with a human, so it takes a lot of practice for them to realize that they need to listen to you and follow your lead. A puppy class won't necessarily prepare them for the show ring, but it will give them a good foundation on which to build their training. Also, it gives the owner the opportunity to seek advice from an expert trainer. It's possible to train your dog without formal classes, but they're incredibly useful when working with a new dog.

There are tons of different trainers with different methods. If you do a quick search, you'll find trainers who conduct lessons at their home, trainers who work out of pet stores, and some that train dogs at a dog club. Any of these options are fine. When choosing a trainer, look for one that uses training methods that coincide with your values for your pup. For example, if you want to focus on using positive-only techniques, and you find a trainer that is stern and uses punishments, it's probably not a good pick. Choose a trainer that is knowledgeable and has a good reputation within the community or the club they work for.

Supplies

Before you bring your dog home, you should already have the necessary supplies on hand so you don't have to leave your dog at home alone to go shopping. It may seem like you're buying a ton of things all at once, but remember, some of these supplies will last you the entirety of your dog's life.

First, you'll need a sturdy collar and leash. A flat, buckled collar is good for daily use. You'll want something that fits snugly but is comfortable for your dog to wear every day. On this collar, you'll want to put a personalized tag on the front loop in case your dog gets lost and needs to be identified. When it comes to leashes, a four- or six-foot leash is all you'll need. Retractable leashes are popular, but they make it hard to control your dog. A strong, nylon leash that can withstand your dog's strength is perfect.

Next, you'll need dishes, food, and treats. Because Cockapoos have floppy ears, they get infected easily when they get wet. An elevated water dish allows them to drink water without it getting into their ears. Pet stores sell food and water dish platforms that lift the dishes far enough off the ground to prevent this problem. Or you might even decide to make one yourself! A good puppy formula is important for giving your Cockapoo the nutrients they need to grow into healthy adults. Later chapters will cover food and nutrition. Treats are vital to keep on hand at all times. A good treat can transform your Cockapoo from a wild animal into a perfect canine citizen. If you want to train your dog to do anything, you'll need to have some tasty treats.

Toys and chews are also important for your dog's upbringing. Cockapoos are extremely playful and love to have a good time. A variety of sturdy toys can keep their interest for hours, preventing them from acting out from boredom. You don't have to spoil your dog rotten, but a good selection of toys will make your best friend very happy. Choose a toy that's fun to chase around the yard, like a ball or a Frisbee, something that is interactive, like a tug rope, something that works their mind, like a food puzzle, and some-

thing that gives into their animal instinct, like a squeaky toy. These basics will keep your dog from getting tired of the same old games every day.

It's also necessary for your dog to have something to chew on. Otherwise, they will gnaw on everything you own. It's only natural for dogs, especially puppies, to chew. It calms them down and keeps their mind busy. Teething puppies need to chew because it helps them work their new teeth through their gums. Choose a size-appropriate chew toy that won't break or splinter into small pieces that can be choked on. Pet stores sell different types of real and synthetic bones and animal materials to keep your dog busy.

Next, you'll need grooming supplies. A Cockapoo's fur needs to be brushed regularly to keep from getting matted. Because they don't shed a lot of fur and have a single coat, a basic pin brush should be enough to keep your dog's fur tangle-free and shiny. It might also be a good idea to keep a bottle of dog shampoo on hand in case your pup gets into something dirty or stinky. If you plan on cutting your dog's toenails, a good set of clippers will come in handy. Find a pair that cut the nail instead of crushing it. Some clippers even come with a guard that prevents you from cutting too much of the nail off if your dog gets squirmy. A toothbrush and toothpaste are also necessary for your dog's oral health. Pet stores sell brushes that are specially designed to fit a dog's mouth and come with toothpaste with dog-friendly flavors, like poultry or peanut butter.

Finally, you'll need a crate, a bed, or both for your dog's relaxation and security. A soft dog bed is a good place for your dog to chill out while she's hanging out with the family. Find one that's the right size for your Cockapoo and make sure it has plenty of padding. Crates also make excellent sleeping spots. When it comes to picking the right size, choose one large enough for your dog to be able to turn around in circles, but not so big that they can roam around. It should be like a cozy den, not a small room.

How Much Will This Cost?

All of these pet supplies can add up very quickly. When you start to factor how much your dog is going to cost you, it's enough to make your head spin. For this reason, it's important to budget for your new pet. Barring any medical complications, the first year of their life will probably be the most expensive for you. You'll have to buy all new supplies and take frequent visits to the vet for checkups and shots. Once you learn your Cockapoo's preferences, you'll be able to buy foods and treats in bulk, and you won't waste your time buying toys and chews your dog doesn't play with.

Prices for supplies and services vary from place to place. Also, it makes a huge difference in the budget if you buy a super expensive dog food compared to a bargain brand one. This estimation of how much your Cockapoo will cost in the first year of his life should be used as a general guide to give you an idea of how much you may need to spend. Of course, location and choices make a big difference in cost, but hopefully, you'll start to figure out how to budget for your pup.

First of all, to buy a Cockapoo from a good breeder, you will likely spend anywhere from $1,000 to $1,500. If you choose to adopt, you're looking at somewhere around $100 to$200, which often includes spay/neuter surgery, shots, and micro-chipping. If you buy your dog, a spay/neuter surgery is, on average, around $75.

Yearly veterinary costs will be around $200 to $500 a year for basic services. Not all vaccines are required on a yearly basis, so some visits will cost more than others. You'll also need to budget at least $100 on heartworm medication and flea and tick preventative.

Next, you'll have to buy many bags of dog food during the course of a year. The average dog eats about $400 worth of dog food per year.

Depending on which size of Cockapoo you get, you may get away with spending less than average. You'll also need lots of treats for training purposes, which will cost you about $100 a year.

Then, we have all the supplies you'll buy right away. Leashes, grooming equipment, and dishes will add up. You'll also need some fun toys and chews for your dog. In total, you're looking at spending approximately $200 around the time you bring your dog home.

It's hard to estimate how much your dog will cost you, but you could spend around $1,000 the first year, not including the dog. Over a dog's lifetime, it's said that the average person spends around $10,000 on their pup. This seems like a lot of money now, but once you get your dog adjusted into their new home, you'd spend all of your money to make your dog happy.

All of this preparation probably seems overwhelming, but you'll feel much better compared to if you didn't plan at all. It may seem like dogs require a lot of things, but they mostly just need the basics and lots of love and attention from you. In no time, you'll find yourself spoiling your little Cockapoo rotten with the best toys and the tastiest treats. After all, your Cockapoo is a member of your family now, and you'd do anything to treat them like your own.

Photo Courtesy of Glenda Stickler

CHAPTER 5
Puppy Parenting

"Two simple things are required to get a new puppy/dog. Love & patience, if you can do both of those two things, then you will do great and everything will fall into place!"

Daxon Weaver

Weaver Family Farms

Once your Cockapoo puppy is adjusted to their new home, it's time to get to work. Puppies require a little discipline so that they can grow up to be awesome adult dogs and not tiny terrors. Your aim is to be consistent, but gentle, while you show your dog how things work around your household. In the end, your Cockapoo pup will know exactly what you expect from them and will feel even more like a member of the family.

Photo Courtesy of Carolyn Long

Standing By Your Expectations

When starting out, it's so easy to come up with a list of expectations for your puppy, just to loosen the slack once you find out how much work it is to train your dog. Resist this urge to become complacent at the sight of your puppy's sweet face. You don't need to be a drill sergeant with your Cockapoo, but it's beneficial to have a clear set of rules that don't have exceptions.

For example, you may decide that you never want your dog to sleep on your bed. It's understandable that you'd want one place in your home to be clean and dog-free. So, when your puppy tries to jump on the bed, you shoo them off and teach them not to jump up there. But then you might decide that you want your pup to jump up there so you can take cute pictures on your nice bedspread. This change in the rules confuses your dog and makes them think that maybe it's okay to jump on the bed. Then, they're utterly confused when you shoo them off again later and get mad when they leave dirty paw prints on your bedding.

Dogs don't understand conditions like humans do. They can understand hard and fast rules (bed is forbidden), but they don't understand exceptions to the rules (bed is okay, only when the owner wants to take pictures). Because of this, if you make a rule for your dog, you should stick to it. Dogs do well with routine and consistency.

Crate Training

Crate training is an often-misunderstood practice that can be really beneficial to both you and your dog. Don't think of it as locking your dog in puppy prison; crates should be used to keep your dog comfortable and safe. When used correctly, a crate, or kennel, is a comfy spot to curl up and relax. It can double as a dog bed, with sturdy walls to make your dog feel protected. It's meant to be a place for your dog to sleep through the night and hang out for a few hours at a time otherwise.

Where owners go wrong is when they use it too much. Some will use it in place of human supervision and lock their dog up all day while they're at work or when the dog is misbehaving. This is not an ideal use because it teaches your dog that the crate is a bad place to go, and it could create anxiety in a Cockapoo. If your dog hates going in their crate, it has lost its utility as a safe spot for your dog to go when they get stressed.

It's normal for a puppy to be a bit wary of the crate at first, so it's your job to get them accustomed to hanging out inside. Never push them in; instead, give them space to explore on their own. Put a comfortable blanket inside and toss a tasty treat in there for your dog to snag on their own time. Do this a few times until they're ready to go inside. Next, practice spending longer quantities of time in the crate by putting food and water dishes inside. Your puppy will come to associate food time (good) with spending time in the crate. As your puppy becomes accustomed to hanging out in their crate, try closing the front gate and extend the amount of time you leave them in there. Your goal is to go a whole night without any issues.

Chewing

Especially with puppies, chewing is a necessary activity for dogs. It keeps them calm and entertained as well as cleans their teeth. Puppies will chew regardless if you want them to or not. So, it's best to redirect them from chewing on whatever they find lying around to a more suitable chew toy.

Inevitably, you will catch your Cockapoo chewing on something they shouldn't. When they do this, get their attention. You might clap loudly or say "hey" or "no" in a loud and firm voice. When they're distracted, give them a chew toy and let them continue with their appropriate chewing.

This kind of training requires you to constantly supervise your puppy. You must be watching them in order to correct their mistakes in the moment, because if you discover one of your items with old tooth marks, the teachable moment has passed. Catch your dog in the act, get their attention, and redirect them to a more appropriate item. And if all else fails, pet stores sell sprays that can be applied to furniture that are supposed to taste terrible to dogs. That kind of deterrent may help you if you turn your back on your dog for a moment.

When choosing a dog chew, make sure it's something appropriate for their size. If it's too big, a small Cockapoo won't be interested in gnawing on it. If the toy is too small, it can become a choking hazard for your dog. Pick a toy that will not break into small pieces easily. You might even consider buying different chews to keep your dog interested in chewing on bones and uninterested in chewing on your belongings.

Along with chewing, you will find that your puppy will try to bite you at one point or another. They don't do this because they want to hurt you, but because that's how they play with their puppy siblings. Over time, they'll learn how hard they can mouth another dog before it's painful, but as a puppy, they don't know that their teeth can hurt.

To correct this issue, act like a fellow puppy. If a puppy bites their brother too hard, it will respond with a yelp that signifies that the puppy caused pain. If your dog bites you, let out a high-pitched yelp or "ouch". They'll be surprised by this and will stop biting you, if only for a moment. Continue this every time their sharp puppy teeth nibble you, and they'll finally figure out that their teeth can hurt others.

Barking

Vocalizations are a dog's way of communicating with others. Your dog might bark to warn you that there's someone at the door because they sense a stranger and they want to protect you. However, it can get very annoying if your dog is constantly yapping at seemingly nothing. If you live in an apartment, it's important to teach your dog how to be quiet so you don't drive the rest of your building crazy. However, overriding your dog's natural instinct to bark at stimuli is easier said than done.

One way to deal with barking is just to eliminate all barking triggers. If your dog barks when your front blinds are open, simply shut the blinds and see if that helps. Your dog may be trying to communicate to you that they see something out there that you should be aware of (though they don't know that you're not interested in neighborhood stray cats). A doorbell is another big trigger for dogs because something exciting happens when they hear it. If your dog is a doorbell barker, teach them to lie on their bed or in their kennel when they hear the noise. This might keep them too busy to bark.

Some trainers even suggest that the best way to teach your dog not to bark is to teach them to bark on command. That way, they learn that they must be commanded to bark, and they'll understand the "no bark" command easier. However, these commands can be tough to teach to a puppy.

Another option is to get your dog's attention whenever they bark and surprise them into silence. For example, when your dog begins to bark, clap loudly or shake a bottle of pebbles. The sound will be so surprising that they'll stop barking for a second to figure out what's going on. When they're quiet, praise them and give them a treat. This will let them know that you like it when they're quiet.

Photo Courtesy of
Vicki Kelly

Separation Anxiety

Separation anxiety is a very real possibility with a Cockapoo. They're very family-oriented, companion-minded, sensitive creatures, so they don't like to be away from their people for very long. When they are apart from you, they can get so upset that they act out. While anxiety in dogs may take the form of crying and whining, it can cause your puppy to turn into a tornado of destruction, ripping apart furniture and going potty on the floor.

There are a few things you can do for your Cockapoo to minimize their separation anxiety. One of the biggest things you can do is be mindful of the way you exit and enter your home. If you say goodbye to your dog every time you leave and make a big show of it, it's going to get the dog wound up before you leave him alone for several hours. Or if you return from your day at work and get excited and talk in a high-pitched voice, this shows your dog that it's a big deal for you to return. Over time, this puts them on edge when you leave because they know it's serious for you not to be home. It's really fun to see your dog get excited when you come home, but the best thing you can do is act like nothing exciting is happening. Leave in the morning without hugging your dog goodbye, and return in the afternoon in a calm manner. If you pretend like there's nothing to you leaving and returning, your dog will get the idea that this is normal and there's nothing to worry about.

Another thing you can do is practice spending time apart from your dog and working up a tolerance for time spent alone. For example, if you usually let your dog ride along with you to the grocery store, leave them at home while you're gone for a little bit. When you return without incident, they'll start to understand that there's nothing to be worried about when you're away. Over time, prolong your absence until they can go a full workday without causing destruction.

Bedtime

The night can be a difficult time for your new Cockapoo puppy. They're used to being the center of attention all day, and then you ask them to be quiet for eight hours so you can get some sleep. This can be a little strange and confusing for a puppy that has been on their own schedule for they're whole life thus far.

You may decide that it's best for your dog to sleep somewhere near you so they know you haven't abandoned them. This also allows you to hear when they need to go to the bathroom in the middle of the night. However, this arrangement might not be a permanent option, as dogs tend to do things like lick themselves and scratch in the middle of the night, which can disrupt a light sleeper. As your puppy ages, start increasing the space between you and your dog at night.

Sometimes your puppy will not want to settle down when you're ready for bed, or they'll wake up and want to play shortly after retiring. To mitigate this issue, make sure your dog gets plenty of exercise before bed. Maybe go

Photo Courtesy of Mel Shaw

to the park or go on a walk in the evening to burn a bunch of energy, and then cuddle with your dog right before bed to calm them down. That way, they aren't full of pent-up energy, but they aren't still excited from playtime either.

It's also important to make sure your puppy goes potty immediately before bedtime. Their tiny bladders can only hold so much, so to increase the amount of time between potty breaks, you'll have to get them to go before bed. Using the bathroom before bed will help them get into a routine. They'll understand that going out at night is for their bathroom break, and then they'll settle down and go to sleep once they're inside.

Home Alone

A well-behaved adult Cockapoo can be trusted to stay home alone for a few hours, but puppies are another story. Puppies like to get into mischief and go to the bathroom where they please. If you have to leave your puppy home alone, here are a few tips and ideas for minimizing potential disasters.

Make sure your Cockapoo gets as much exercise as possible throughout the day. If you work away from home, take your dog for a quick walk in the morning to wake them up and get them moving. When you leave for the day, leave out fun puzzle toys for your dog to work at. This will keep them busy for a little while so they won't get bored. Chew toys are also great for entertaining your dog and they don't require your supervision. If you come home for lunch or have a sitter let your dog out, use this time to throw a ball and get your dog moving again. If your dog is tired, they are less likely to become anxious and may even nap while you're gone.

If you have issues with your puppy going potty in the house while you're gone, hiring a dog walker gives your dog the opportunity to go outside to use the bathroom midday. This means that you have fewer accidents to clean up when you get home, and your dog won't be so worried about being alone all day.

A new puppy takes a lot of work. It's easy to get frustrated at their behaviors, but they're still learning to assimilate to your household and your rules. It takes a little time for them to learn how to be a dog and how to be a pet. Be patient and stick to your training. In the end, all of your hard work in puppy raising will pay off when you have a great adult Cockapoo. Also, don't forget to enjoy your time as a puppy parent. Before you know it, your little puppy will be a grown dog!

Photo Courtesy of
Lorraine Owen

CHAPTER 6
Housetraining

"When housetraining your Cockapoo puppy, take note of the puppy's favorite places to relieve itself. Strategically place puppy pads or potty training pads in those favorite potty places. In addition, remember that a puppy will almost immediately urinate when it wakes up from a nap, so be prepared to pick the puppy up immediately and take him or her outside."

Alisa Foerderer
Foerderer Horses and Cock-a-poos

When you bring your new puppy home, housetraining is perhaps the top priority on your mind. Learning how to sit and stay can wait, because it's less than ideal to have little puddles of puppy pee on the carpet. It's said that a puppy can only hold their potty, in hours, for as many months are they are old. So, if your puppy is two months old, they can reasonably hold it for two hours. That keeps you on a very tight schedule of letting your dog outside to see if they need to go. Sometimes, they'll walk around on the grass and do nothing, but the second you bring them inside, they use the bathroom on your kitchen floor. It's an annoying and messy process to housetrain your dog, but if you use every moment as a lesson, you'll be past that stage in no time.

*Photo Courtesy of
Julie Blakeway*

Different Options for Potty Training

Photo Courtesy of Sarah Vaughan

When it comes to places you let your dog go to the bathroom, outside is best. Cleaning up is easy and doesn't leave an odor behind for you to deal with. But it's not always possible to get your dog to go to the bathroom outside every single time. There are some options when it comes to housetraining.

Cockapoos are unique because they come in a wide range of sizes. If you have a mini or toy Cockapoo, their messes will be much smaller than a standard Cockapoo's. This makes the smaller versions perfect for apartment dwellers. But if you do live in an apartment, it's not so easy to find the perfect patch of grass every time your pup needs to potty. That's where potty pads and grass mats come into play.

There are products specifically designed to help little dogs do their business inside without causing a mess for you. Potty pads are absorbent sheets that you can lay on top of your floor. They contain special enzymes and smells that make your dog want to potty on it. When your dog feels the urge to go, they'll wander over to the potty pad instead of your couch. When their business is finished, all you have to do is throw the pad away. Think of it like a diaper for a dog. Even if you don't plan on indoor potty training your dog, these might be nice to have on hand, especially at night.

There are also products that are a cross between a litter box and the outdoors. These contraptions consist of a small frame with artificial grass (or real grass) inside. You teach our dog to use the mat, just as you would teach them to go potty outside. With enough practice, they'll divert all important business to their designated spot. You'll still have to clean up the mess when you get home, but at least all of the mess will be in one spot. This method is useful for owners of small dogs who cannot take them outside at their every whim.

There are some downfalls for teaching your dog to use the potty inside. While it can be very convenient, it's not ideal to have pet waste in your home. If you have a small space, the scent will eventually fill the air no matter how much cleaning you do. Also, it might be nice to have an indoor option to prevent accidents, but it might be harder to teach your dog to hold it until you get outside when he's a little older and has more control. The adjustment to the outside-only potty may be a bigger struggle than you initially anticipated.

The First Few Weeks

"I always tell people to immediately start with potty training. Cockapoos are incredibly smart so the more time you spend training them the better. Positive reinforcement and repetition are key to getting your puppy trained in a timely manner."

Jamie
Cute Cockapoos

Photo Courtesy of
Linda Bareham

If you're buying your puppy from a breeder, you'll likely have your Cockapoo in your hands around the time they are two months old. This means that your puppy will want to eat and drink all the time to feed their growing body. This also causes them to turn into little waste-making machines that have very little control over their body.

Unfortunately for the owner, this means that you'll be spending a lot of those first few weeks either outside or cleaning up messes. Don't worry—with proper training, this stage will get much easier. Until then, stay vigilant about keeping an eye on your puppy.

If your puppy needs to go to the bathroom every two hours, this doesn't mean that you can set a timer for every two hours to make your trips. Your puppy does not run on an exact schedule, and accidents are bound to happen if they don't have the opportunity to go. Instead, plan to go out every hour, if possible. Walk them to their designated potty spot in your yard and let them sniff around. If they don't go, head right back inside and try again later.

You may feel like you're going outside way too often, but you'll find that you'll have fewer accidents if you maximize the opportunities for your dog to go potty.

Rewarding Positive Behavior

Cockapoos are sensitive dogs that respond well to positive reinforcement. Potty training is one of those high-stress moments that will test your patience. However, it's very important to keep your cool. Acting out in anger will confuse your poor pup and set them back in their training.

It's a common misconception that you can discourage your dog from having accidents by rubbing their nose in it. This is a harmful practice that will only make things harder on you and your dog. Dogs do not remember things in the same way humans do. If your dog has an accident and you find it after the fact, rubbing their nose in it and getting angry does not help them remember that what they did was forbidden. Instead, they'll associate their bodily function with your anger. This will lead to more accidents in hidden places because they think you'll get angry if they potty at all.

This means that you can only teach them in moments you are present for. If you find a mess when you come home from work, the only thing you can do is clean it up and try to be there for the next time your dog has to go. If you catch your dog in the process of going to the bathroom in your home, call attention to it. Clap your hands to get your dog's attention and make the effort to get them outside before they go. Over time, you'll start to learn your dog's cues that they need to go. Every time you get them outside to their special spot before they have an accident is a success and a teachable moment. Punishing them for something they did while you were not around will only cause more unwanted behavior.

Because this dog responds to positivity, you'll want to make your dog feel like the best dog in the world if they potty outside. Every single time they go to the bathroom outside, give them all the praise and affection you can. Keep yummy treats on hand to give them when their business is complete. This will reinforce the idea that they're supposed to go to the bathroom outside, so much so that the thought of going inside and not getting any treats or praise is unappealing. If your dog is play-driven, toss a ball around for a few minutes after a successful trip outside. Whatever you do, make sure they know you love it when they can make it outside to go potty.

When an accident happens, make sure to clean up the mess thoroughly. The smell of dog urine sticks around for a long time. That's why you'll notice that your dog goes to the same place in the yard almost every time. This smell signals them to return to their little bathroom time and time again. So, if you don't remove the odor from your home, they will come to know that spot as their indoor bathroom. Scrubbing will only get you so far, so remember to use a special pet mess cleaner that's designed to remove the enzymes that mark their territory. Otherwise, you'll find yourself cleaning up the same spot again and again.

Crate Training for Housetraining (and Other Tricks)

A crate is a wonderful tool that can be used for many reasons. If you are training your puppy to sleep in their crate, this can help cut down on accidents at night.

Though you may believe otherwise when your dog tears through your home, dogs are neat creatures when it comes to their own personal space. Generally, dogs dislike using the bathroom in their den. As long as the crate isn't too big for your dog, they're not going to want to go to the bathroom in there unless it is an emergency. They are more likely to wait until you let them out to go to the bathroom than they are to potty in their kennel if they can help it. This makes the crate a great place to keep them during the night. And if they do end up having an accident, you'll know exactly where you need to clean because it will all be contained within a small space.

Photo Courtesy of Liam Thompson

If you don't want to crate train, you'll still want to limit the amount of space they have when you're not able to supervise them. A pen works well for these types of instances. If the space is confined enough, they will be less likely to soil their sleeping location. When you are home, give your dog plenty of room to roam around and explore. But if you have to leave for a bit, put your puppy in the pen to keep their messes under control.

Some owners also install doggie doors in hopes that their pups will be able to go outside and take care of their own business while their person is away. This can be a very helpful tool for people with a fenced-in backyard and a responsible puppy. However, if your dog requires a little more supervision, think about if you want your dog to be able to go in and out on their own accord. Puppies are adventurous creatures, and you may change your mind about the doggie door once they hunt their first baby animal and leave it for you as a present!

Especially in the first few months, you might find yourself wishing you had purchased an adult dog. Don't despair; the worst of your puppy training will soon be over. Then, you'll look back and miss the days that your puppy was so small! During this period, try to spend as much time as you can supervising your dog so you can create as many teaching moments as possible. If your dog has accidents (and they will) keep calm and clean it up. When your dog successfully uses the bathroom outside, let your dog know how loved she is. With lots of repetition, your Cockapoo will eventually get the hang of house-training and you'll never have to worry about an accident again.

CHAPTER 7
Socialization

Socialization is such an important part of raising a well-adjusted dog, but it is often forgotten about. With so many books and classes that talk about formal obedience training, owners forget there is more to a good dog than being able to sit when told.

When it comes to your dog, socialization is the ability of your dog to get along with others. This includes other people and dogs. This process is best done when your puppy is around 4-7 months old, but you can still work on socialization skills at any age. Cockapoos are usually friendly towards others, but your dog will still require a lot of practice around others.

Photo Courtesy of Carolyn Young

The Importance of Socialization

When you go out in public, you want your dog to be calm and get along with other people and dogs. You don't want your dog to be fearful or aggressive when a stranger wants to pet your Cockapoo. A trip to the dog park can be a nightmare if your dog can't get along with others. If your dog is not socialized, you'll find that you can't take them out in public because they won't respond well. You'll worry about how your dog will react if you have friends over. With a poorly socialized dog, it'll be hard to add another dog to your household in the future. In short, your life and your dog's life will be tougher if you don't take the time to socialize your pooch properly.

Cockapoos aren't typically fearful dogs, but they are sensitive. Sometimes, this sensitivity can manifest as fear if they're unable to make sense of the world around them. Your job as an owner is to help them apply some context to the things they see or hear. You want to show your dog that the world isn't so scary and that the things they're experiencing are perfectly safe.

Your attitude matters when it comes to keeping your dog calm. Dogs can pick up on non-verbal cues very well. Your posture, the tension on the leash, and even the tone of your voice send messages to your dog. For example, a soft, low voice may signal that you're calm. A stern voice can signal that you're not messing around. A high-pitched voice relays a message of anxiety or excitement. Some trainers say that your dog can read you through the leash. This is to say, if you're guiding your dog, think about the slight cues you're sending to your pup.

Treats are also very helpful when it comes to teaching your dog that something is okay. Dogs learn through conditioning, so if they're rewarded for specific behaviors, they will associate the action with the reward.

For example, maybe your dog gets nervous at dog parks and wants to run back to the car right after you get past the gate. You want your dog to be able to get exercise and play with other dogs, so you need to change their perception that the dog park is a scary place. When you get to the park, you might give your dog a treat for getting out of the car and staying calm. You can give your dog another treat when they make it to the gate, or they go inside and turn around and run. Every little step that your dog takes to face their fear, they get a reward for staying calm. With enough practice (and treats,) they should get to the point where they associate the formerly scary thing with an awesome reward.

Fear of everyday occurrences, like hanging around strangers or other dogs, is not good for your Cockapoo. Not only does stress negatively affect your dog's overall well-being, but it can be dangerous to others. Fear is not always expressed as cowering in the corner or hiding under

Photo Courtesy of
Jackie Meredith

the bed. Fear can be a dog on the edge that is willing to attack just to protect themselves from a perceived danger. A dog might not know how to
play with other dogs, so when a friendly dog comes up to roughhouse
with your dog, your dog might panic and attack because they haven't had
the proper experiences. Or if a child runs up to your dog and wants to pet
them on the head, your pooch may snap at their little hands because they
don't know what's going to happen to them. In either case, your dog cannot learn that fighting back is an acceptable response to new experiences.
The last thing you want is for your dog to hurt another human or animal.

But, if you expose your dog to enough different experiences in a positive manner, your dog will be less likely to act out of fear. Take your dog to
different places and let them interact with different people and animals.
Make them feel comfortable by keeping calm and behaving like everything
is normal. Bring treats along and reward your dog when they're relaxed and
responding to you. Start slow and let your dog hang out with one other dog
or invite a friend over to meet your dog. If that goes well, increase the number of new people your dog meets. As long as your dog is doing well, increase the stakes until you're comfortable with your dog being anywhere.

Of course, try not to push your dog if they're not ready. It can be
frustrating if your dog can't get along with others, but forcing them to do
something they really don't want to do for the sake of progress can be
dangerous. You may understand that your dog isn't in any real danger,
but they don't understand that until they learn otherwise.

Behavior Around Other Dogs

While you may be confident that your Cockapoo is a precious angel who would never hurt a fly, you may not be so sure about all the other dogs out there. It's normal to be concerned about your dog when introducing them to other pups, but you have to keep your anxiety to a minimum for the sake of your dog. Otherwise, they will learn to be hesitant around others, too. Part of socialization practice is learning how to behave around your dog while they are learning how to behave around other dogs!

For your dog's safety, keep the dogs on leashes to start. That way, if a scuffle erupts, you can quickly separate the dogs and lead them to a space for them to calm down. But, this doesn't mean that you have to keep a tight leash and stand close to your dog while they sniff the other dogs. Give them their space and allow them to walk to the end of the leash to greet the other dog. It can be a natural reaction to have one hand on your dog to reassure them, but unless they're in danger, they can be given some space to socialize.

If that goes well, you can let your dog off their leash and let them play. As you'll find out, letting your dog run around with a friend is a great way for them to get the exercise and mental stimulation they need. Again, give your dog a little space, but watch all dogs involved for cues that things are headed in a rough direction.

For a new dog owner, it can be hard to distinguish between play behaviors and fighting behaviors. If you freak out and jump in when your

*Photo Courtesy of
Sarah Johnson*

Photo Courtesy of Morrigan Harvey

dog is just playing rough, you'll create some confusion.

As a general rule, if your dog is wagging their tail, that's a good sign. Dogs will also make a bowing motion towards other dogs that is like an invitation to play. Dogs will occasionally make biting motions towards another dog's neck, but this is done with a gentle mouth. You may even find that your dog isn't really making contact, but almost "pretend biting" at their friend. These are all cues that your dog is happy and having fun.

You'll need to watch out for the signs that your dog's not having a great time. These include sounds, such as snarling, snapping, and whimpering. A tail between the legs is another good sign that your dog is afraid. Bared teeth and raised hairs on the back of their neck are a sign that they're about to become aggressive. Because a fight with a dog can set their socialization back, try to intervene before things get too out of hand.

If your dog rolls over on their back and exposes their belly to another dog, it's a way of surrendering. This is a sign that your dog is not very comfortable with their role in the group of dogs. This signals to other dogs that your pup is not interested in their games and does not want to challenge anyone. The other dogs should understand this sign and leave your dog alone, as it is clear they do not want to participate in play.

If your dog does well with their socialization practice, make sure to reward them. But, you'll probably find that being able to play with a friend is enough of a reward for them. Even if you don't spend a lot of time around other dogs in your regular schedule, it's still important for your dog to get along with others. You never know when an opportunity will arise where your dog needs to be able to behave around others of his own kind. Because socialization is most effectively done while the dog is a puppy, you don't want to regret not taking your dog to the dog park for practice while you had the chance.

Properly Greeting New People

Unless you and your Cockapoo live under a rock, your dog will interact with other humans frequently. Whether your dog needs to greet a friend or the mailperson, you'll want them to be on their best behavior. But if your sensitive dog is occasionally anxious, they may be wary of a new smell and unfamiliar face. So it's important to teach them that it's okay to interact with all types of people.

Socialization with people is similar to socializing with dogs, but hopefully, people will be easier for you to control. If your puppy is a little nervous, it's a good idea to let strangers know this. That way, they'll approach your dog slowly and gently and not try to give them a big hug when your dog isn't ready for that kind of interaction.

When teaching your dog how to interact with people, have the person come towards your dog and have them offer the back of their hand for your dog to sniff. Have the person move slowly so your dog doesn't think they're about to be grabbed or tricked into doing something they don't want to do. If your dog is curious, let the person give them a treat or pet your dog's back. For some dogs, a head pat is too personal and only reserved for people they trust the most.

One way to get into socialization is to take your dog on a walk at places where you know you'll see other people. Bring treats along and ask passersby to give one of the treats to your dog if they are calm. You'll find that if you explain what you're doing, most people are more than willing to stop for a second to pet your adorable Cockapoo.

Once your dog has mastered this, take them somewhere with more people. Repeat this step until your dog can walk through a crowd without getting nervous. Outdoor shopping centers and farmers markets are great places to test your dog's ability to keep cool. You'll also need to remember that some dogs react differently to different people. For example, if you're a petite woman and your dog has only ever interacted with petite people or women, a large man wanting to pet your dog may freak your dog out. Make sure your dog has positive interactions with all sorts of different people, so when someone who looks a little different comes into your house, your Cockapoo won't panic.

It's best not to wait too long when it comes to the socialization process. Slowly start introducing your dog to other people and dogs in the first six months of their life. Otherwise, it's easy for them to get stuck in their own ways. If you have an adult Cockapoo that is nervous around others, not all hope is lost. You can still integrate your dog into polite society—it might just take a little extra work. Start slowly, be patient, and in no time, your dog will want to be the center of attention, no matter who they're around.

CHAPTER 8
Cockapoos and Your Other Pets

If your new Cockapoo is not your only animal, socialization is much more important than if they were an only pup. When you have other animals in your home all the time, the stakes are much higher for them to get along. Especially if you ever plan to leave your animals alone without any supervision, it's absolutely necessary for them to get along.

Introducing Your Puppy to Other Pets

A good introduction can go a long way. Introduce your new Cockapoo to your new pets before you even bring your dog home. Your old dogs may feel like they need to protect their turf if a new puppy suddenly waltzes in. This can create discord that lingers on, so it's best to make sure everyone is happy from the start.

As stated in the chapter about your puppy's first few weeks, it's good to start this process slow and have your pets meet in neutral territory. A park, a friend's house, or even your breeder's home is a good place to let your pets get to know one another. Then, once they feel comfortable and can behave themselves, let them get acquainted in your home.

During this period, supervision is a must. Your Cockapoo might be just fine when you're watching, but an animal's behavior can change in an instant when their owner isn't looking. Don't be surprised if you leave the room for a minute and come back to a commotion. Because you don't want any of your pets to be harmed by a simple misunderstanding, it's important for someone to be there at all times in the early days.

If you have a dog, this process may go smoothly. After all, your puppy will have spent a little time around other dogs. It's a lot less likely that your new Cockapoo has spent time with a cat, though. It's not impossible for cats and dogs to get along. Many times, they coexist in a home with no issues. However, it's likely that your dog has no idea how to act around a cat, and your cat will not be amused by a little puppy sniffing them and disrupting their peace.

The introduction between your Cockapoo and your cat may be a little different because many cats are generally disinterested in playing with dogs. If you can get them in the same space without a catastrophe, this is a win. Try to let your puppy get a good sniff of the cat so he can figure out what the heck that furry non-dog is, but not so close that he'll get his nose scratched.

Photo Courtesy of
Kelly Collins

With these interactions, you want to be positive that your Cockapoo is not going to think the cat is prey and try to give chase. A dog can seriously injure another animal. Always make sure your cat has an exit strategy if your dog gets too rough. A cat tree is good for keeping your cat out of reach, but a room that your cat can escape to is also great for the early months when your dog hasn't entirely figured out what cats are all about.

Over time, you'll feel more comfortable leaving your pets home alone for short periods of time. Remember to utilize all of the resources you have until then. Gates work well for separating animals that might not get along immediately. Also, pet sitting services or doggy daycares can be used to give your pup a little more supervision until they figure out how they're supposed to behave.

Pack Mentality

Though the dogs of today are far removed from their canine ancestors, a lot of trainers use concepts from how wolf packs operate for domesticated dogs. These rules of order amongst dogs are not hard and fast rules, but they may give you an idea of why your dog acts the way they do.

In a dog pack, there is a leader, or alpha. This alpha keeps the other dogs in line. He is dominant and puts the other dogs in place. Because there is a leader, the other dogs are followers with different degrees of submissiveness. These dogs do not try to take control, but follow along with the pack.

Dominance and submission in dogs is not necessarily a bad thing. People often mistake dominance for aggression and submission for fear. While it's possible for a dog to have both traits, they are not mutually exclusive. Some dogs just feel comfortable in different roles; it does not necessarily mean they are aggressive if they're a leader or a wimp if they're a follower.

Once your dog becomes integrated within their new "pack" of dogs in your home, you'll start to notice a hierarchy develop. One of your dogs may try to take control and make the rules. This is natural and perfectly fine as long as no one is getting hurt.

Remember if your dogs form their own pack with different levels of leadership, you still need to be the alpha dog. When you go on walks with your pack, you choose the direction. When it's suppertime, you should eat first before feeding your dogs. Small gestures show your pups that you're still in charge, even though the pack has new members.

Fighting

Sometimes you do everything right and you still notice your dogs fighting. When this happens, it's important to break it up quickly before things get dangerous. If you're around your dogs, it's likely that you'll notice the signs of an impending fight before it even happens. You may hear growling and see your dog's teeth bared. They will also be making eye contact with the dog they plan on fighting.

The first thing you want to do is to break the eye contact between dogs. It's not always safe to walk in between two dogs ready to brawl, so use your best judgment. Try making a loud noise to break the dogs from their trance. If this doesn't work, try to make a barrier between the two dogs or pull them away—anything to get them to stop staring at each other. Again, be careful, because you don't want to get caught in between two dogs when they start fighting.

Photo Courtesy of
Neil Cauldwell

If you missed the warning signs and the dogs have started to fight, you need to safely separate them. If your dog happens to be on a leash, give a quick tug and lead the dogs away from each other. If they aren't on a leash, grab your dog's back legs and walk them away from the fight like a wheelbarrow. This keeps your hands away from their teeth and temporarily disables them from being an effective fighter. Once the dogs are separated, they need time apart to cool down. Send one dog to the backyard and keep the other one inside. Or, place the dogs in separate rooms so they don't have the opportunity to lock eyes again. When they've spent enough time away, let them return to the same area of the house and watch them closely. With any luck, whatever triggered the fight has been long forgotten. Don't worry about pushing your dogs together to "make up" after a scuffle. In this situation, it's best to just pretend like nothing happened.

The Dangers of Buying Littermates

If one new Cockapoo puppy is good, then two must be great, right? You may have decided that you would like to have two Cockapoos in your home. There's nothing wrong with having two dogs of the same breed and around the same age. These dogs make excellent companions to people and to each other. They can keep each other company and entertain each other while you're not home. But, it's not a good idea to take on multiple puppies from the same litter.

First of all, it's a ton of work to have just one puppy. Now, imagine doubling up on all the work you have to do. That's double the accidents, double the trips outside in the middle of the night, and double the tiny teeth marks on your furniture. It's not impossible to raise two puppies at once, but unless you have a ton of time, energy, and experience raising puppies, it's not ideal.

Also, many dog owners don't realize that owning two siblings from the same litter isn't a good thing. One might think that littermates would get along better than dogs from separate litters, but this is not often the case. Many trainers recommend not buying littermates because they can be difficult to deal with.

This is evident when it comes time to train your dogs. Littermates are often distracted by each other because they're so close. They just don't have the same focus as dogs from different litters do. If you sign up for a class, your trainer might not even let you bring both dogs to the same training session. You'll grow frustrated constantly split your time between pups just to teach them simple commands.

Photo Courtesy of
Marita Boast

Littermates also have increased separation anxiety if they have to be apart. For example, you might need to take one pup to the vet but not the other. In the meantime, both dogs are going to freak out because they're apart from their mate. This anxiety can make them difficult to work with or bring out destructive behaviors.

It's not impossible to raise littermates, but it's definitely not ideal. If you're set on getting two Cockapoos, consider buying one and getting them past the early puppy stage before buying another. This way, you don't have to spend all of your time raising puppies, and they won't suffer from Littermate Syndrome.

What if My Pets Don't Get Along?

It's not uncommon for an owner's pets to not get along with a puppy right away. Perhaps your dogs are older and feel the need to whip your puppy into shape. Or maybe there's something in your dog's DNA that makes it hard for them to get along with other dogs. Whatever the issue is, it's important to get everything settled before one of your pets gets hurt.

Try to create space between your pets. Maybe the issue is that they're cooped up in the same room and have to stare at each other all day. Give them separate parts of the house to hang out in so they don't feel like they're constantly competing for space. Crates and gates can help create distance in a small home. You might even take your dogs on separate walks or take them to separate training classes so they have some time apart (and quality time with you).

If nothing you've tried is working, it's time to come up with a plan to prevent the worst from happening. Consult with a trainer or dog behavioral specialist to meet your dogs and diagnose the problem.

If you absolutely can't keep your pets from fighting, you have a tough decision to make. It can be very hard to give up a dog, but their life may depend on it. If nothing you do is working, a new home for one of your dogs is better than having one get seriously injured by the other.

A Cockapoo can be an excellent addition to your dog-friendly household because the breed is good with other dogs. However, it's important to do whatever you can to make all pets feel loved and taken care of. Slowly work your new Cockapoo into your household so your other pets aren't threatened or confused. Once your new dog is home, watch everyone carefully to prevent altercations. Never force your animals to be together if they don't want to, and give them plenty of options for having their own space. Most importantly, keep calm and allow your dogs the time they need to become friends. If you show your old dogs that a new puppy is a good thing, they'll be more likely to believe you than if you constantly fret and hover over them. In no time, your pup will be the best of friends with the animals you already call family.

CHAPTER 9
Exercise

"Cockapoos are smart and can get bored easily which can lead to naughty behavior. It's vital to spend a lot of time playing with and exercising your puppy."

Jamie

Cute Cockapoos

Photo Courtesy of
Stuart Baynham

When it comes to giving your dog something to do, exercise is non-negotiable. All dogs, no matter their size or breed, require some sort of activity to keep them moving. Daily exercise is an integral part of your dog's physical and mental health. Without it, they can pack on the pounds or even become anxious. Cockapoos are lively dogs, so they'll need an outlet for their energy to be happy and healthy.

The idea of frequent exercise can be daunting, especially if you're not so active yourself! Exercise for a dog doesn't necessarily mean going for a jog, though it's a quick way to burn energy in a hyper pup. Exercise can be a gentle walk, a long game of fetch, or an afternoon at doggy daycare roughhousing with friends. And if you're not in the best shape, a dog is the perfect motivation to get fit.

Cockapoos make great pets because they don't require a ton of exercise compared to other breeds. And the smaller the Cockapoo, the less exercise they will require because a toy Cockapoo's little legs can only go so far. You can still take these dogs on long walks, but they won't require as much exercise as a breed like a Border Collie might. This makes them a good pet for a first-time dog owner or someone with limited space in their home.

*Photo Courtesy of
Adele Donaldson*

Exercise Requirements

Try to get your dog outside a few times during the day. If you have a fenced-in backyard, you can allow your dog to get little spurts of exercise throughout the day. Otherwise, a walk in the morning and evening will suffice. These don't necessarily have to be particularly long walks either. After spending some time with your dog, you'll be able to determine how much exercise they need. A quick morning walk is a great time to get your dog to go to the bathroom after a long night of holding it. It also gives them the opportunity to stretch their legs and spend some time with you after they wait all night for you to wake up.

If your dog suffers from separation anxiety, some strenuous exercise can help them remain calm when you leave the house. A tired dog is the best-behaved dog because they don't have a ton of energy built up inside them. Exercise-starved dogs may be destructive because they don't have a positive outlet for their energy. If your dog is frantic when you leave the house in the morning, it might help to load up the early morning with exercise so your Cockapoo is more likely to rest after you leave for work. A longer walk, a quick jog, or even some time playing fetch will help your dog relax.

Then, in the evening, give your dog plenty of opportunities to play and burn some energy. If you're out of the house all day, they're going to want to play and be right by your side until bedtime. A long walk in the evening can get their legs going to the point where they'll be happy to snuggle next to you for the rest of the evening. In addition, a trip to the dog park or playing games in the backyard will make for one very happy Cockapoo.

When giving your dog exercise, make sure there is plenty of cool water available. Dogs don't sweat like people do, so they can overheat fairly easily. Also, dogs cannot tell you when they're feeling tired. Often, they're just so excited to be out and about that they don't show any signs of exhaustion until they really can't handle any more activity. If you live in a particularly hot location, consider waiting until a cool part of the day to give your dog the bulk of their exercise requirements. Also, if it's a hot and sunny day, feel the concrete with your bare feet. If it's too hot for you to walk without shoes, it's too hot for your dog to walk on the concrete. Dogs hide their discomfort very well, so you may not know your dog is in pain unless symptoms develop. When it comes to extreme weather, be mindful of your dog's comfort.

Photo Courtesy of Anne

Types of Exercise to Try

Dog exercise can be much more than going on walks. Switching up your dog's exercise routine can keep them from getting bored with one activity. There are so many fun things to do with your dog, so it's great to try a wide range of activities to see what your dog enjoys the most.

If you have a backyard or access to another large, grassy space, there are many games you can play to challenge your dog's coordination and skills. Tennis balls are a great toy to toss into the air to get your dog to practice their catching skills, or launch them as far as you can to see how fast your dog can run. Frisbee can also be a challenging game that will work your dog's coordination as well as your own. When choosing back-yard games to play, you'll want to have a variety of toys on hand to keep your dog from getting bored with the same old stuff.

If you live near a body of water, swimming might be something your dog will enjoy. Not all dogs like water, so it's important to let your dog dip their toes in and decide how they feel before tossing them in. If your dog takes to the water like a fish, you might want to invest in a doggy life jack-et to protect your furry friend. Even if your dog is a strong swimmer, they might overexert themselves and find themselves too far from shore. Life vests come in all sizes, so you should be able to find one that fits your

Photo Courtesy of Lee Carpenter

Photo Courtesy of
Karen Bird

Cockapoo. Of course, it's important to remember to dry their ears after a dip because trapped water can lead to infection.

If you enroll in training courses, you may find that your Cockapoo is awesome at organized sports for dogs. Your Cockapoo may not be the fastest or strongest dog out there, but that doesn't mean that they can't participate in fun competitions. These dogs are reasonably easy to train, so you might consider enrolling them in an agility course to test their skills. They'll practice running up and down ramps, weaving through pylons, and sprinting through tunnels. They'll get so much satisfaction in learning how to do the different obstacles and will love how excited you get when they do an awesome job. Most dog clubs offer beginning agility classes that can be a great opportunity to test your dog's ability. Flyball is another dog sport that your Cockapoo might enjoy. This is like a relay race for dogs. Each team has four dogs that take turns relaying a ball from one side of the room to the other. This sport is generally dominated by large, active dog breeds, but that doesn't mean that your Cockapoo can't participate. You might even be able to find a class that allows them to learn the skills they need to play the game.

Especially in the winter months when you might not be able to go outside very often, a membership to a dog club or an indoor dog park can be very beneficial. Your dog may have more energy in the cooler months, but if they don't have somewhere to go to burn that energy, they will come up with their own destructive games. A facility for dogs is nice for getting your dog out of the house and moving, especially when the weather is not suited for walks.

Mental Exercise

Photo Courtesy of Mandy Watson

Many dog owners don't take into account the mental energy their pooch has. With intelligent breeds like Cockapoos, it's necessary to make sure their minds are being worked as hard as their bodies. Intelligent breeds are fun to work with, but if they don't get the stimulation they need, they can become naughty. Because they get bored easily, they will make up their own games if they don't get what they need from you. These games often involve the destruction of your belongings because they're using whatever they can find as entertainment. If you have to leave your dog alone for any length of time, it's a good idea to make sure their minds are attended to as well as their physical needs.

Fortunately, there are a lot of products out there that can help you with this task. Try out a few different "food puzzles" for your pooch. The original Kong is a popular choice because it's fun for dogs of all abilities. This is a rubber toy that's something between a ball and a cone that can be filled with cheese, peanut butter, or little treats. Because of the toy's shape, it requires a little work to get the treats to fall out. Your dog will need to use their brain to figure out how to lick, toss, or drop the toy to get the treat out. Another food-driven toy, often used for fast eaters, is a ball that can be filled with their kibble. They must push the ball around with their nose to get a few pieces to fall out. One meal could take them thirty minutes of play to finish.

If your dog is looking for a challenge, there are puzzle boards that can be filled with treats to entice your dog to figure out how the contraption works. There are so many varieties out there, but many will require your dog to slide plastic disks, open drawers, and pull levers to get their prize. Raise the stakes and hide the highest-value treat you have to motivate them to work. When your Cockapoo has mastered one, try a new toy with different obstacles.

Training is also a good way to keep your dog's brain active. As long as you make training fun, your dog will enjoy learning and practicing new commands. If you spend 10 to 20 minutes a day working on commands, you'll be amazed at how many cool tricks your pup can learn. This makes them feel like they have a job and a purpose, which will prevent them from using that time for destructive behavior.

Especially when the weather prevents you from going outside, you might want to try to play hide and seek with your dog. Once they learn how to sit and stay, place them in one part of your house. In the meantime, hide in a different room and call them. Wait until they sniff you out, and then give them treats and praise. Repeat this until they get tired of the game. A variation of this game is to hide toys around the house and command them to find their toy. If they get good at this, you can try to teach your dog the names of several toys and command them to retrieve a specific one by name.

Tug is another activity that combines physical and mental exercise. Hand your dog one end of a rope toy and have them pull on the other end. It won't take long for your dog to figure out what to do. Wiggle the rope back and forth and try to trick them into letting up and allowing you to win. This will challenge them to outwit you and win the toy. Some dogs get pretty riled up with this game, so make sure your dog knows that you're in control. Always be the one to initiate the game and let them know when the game is over.

There are so many activities you can do with your Cockapoo that will keep them happy and healthy. Aim for at least thirty minutes of physical exercise and thirty minutes of mental exercise a day. Of course, your dog will want to play as much as possible. Especially in warm weather, keep an eye on your dog and watch for signs of exhaustion. Avoid pushing your dog beyond their capability.

Exercise doesn't have to be a chore for the owner, either. Having a dog is a great excuse to explore different places and to spend time out in nature. Your dog will enjoy getting out to see and smell new things, and you can relax while getting some gentle exercise. Your dog will love spending quality time with you, and you'll enjoy making your pooch as happy as can be!

CHAPTER 10
Training Your Cockapoo

"Schedule is very important, animals especially dogs run on nature's clock, when you choose a schedule roll with it and try to not change it! They will learn very quickly over time when it is time to go outside to use the bathroom, what time is chow time, and when it is bed time!"

Daxon Weaver

Weaver Family Farms

Photo Courtesy of Lucy Russell

One of the most important things you can do for your dog is obedience train them early in their life. There are many benefits to good training, but perhaps the most important is that it will make both you and your pup happy. It's easy to come up with a bunch of training plans in the early days, only to become complacent as life gets in the way. However, your relationship with your dog depends on their understanding of your expectations and their good behavior. Without training, your Cockapoo is just an animal.

If this is your first dog, it's easy to get overwhelmed. You might find that it's simple to get your dog to sit, but impossible to get them to walk on a leash. When your dog is misbehaving, it's too easy to get frustrated and want to give up. Stick with it! Some dogs need a little extra time with certain commands and behaviors. Positivity and patience will get you far when it comes to dog training.

Clear Expectations

In the beginning, decide what you want from your Cockapoo. This is totally up to you as the owner and your preference when it comes to their pet. You may decide that you want your dog to be able to compete in obedience competitions. Or you may just want your dog to be able to sit and stay when needed. Whatever you decide, come up with reasonable expectations for training. If you don't have the time to take classes or practice at home, it's not very reasonable to expect your dog to have perfect behavior. Or if you get angry at your dog every time they mess up, it's unlikely that they will want to learn new tricks. Understand that it will take a lot of time and effort into turning your new Cockapoo into a polite member of society.

Operant Conditioning Basics

Though it may appear that your dog can understand everything you tell him, dogs do not understand what we say like a human child might. When you're training a dog, they don't necessarily hear a command and know why you want them to do that thing. Instead, it's more of a knee-jerk reaction from practicing so many times. If you're familiar with basic psychological concepts, you'll know that dogs are trained through operant conditioning.

In short, operant conditioning requires a response for every action, either positive or negative. One classic demonstration of operant conditioning is done with rats in cages. A cage is outfitted with a lever. Obviously, the rat has never experienced levers before and doesn't know what to do with one. Eventually, the rat will meander over and push the lever. When this happens, a piece of food falls out. The rat will come to understand that every time they push the lever, they get food. Soon, they'll do nothing but work the lever until their little bellies are full of treats.

On the other hand, a second lever might be introduced. This one gives the rats a little shock when they push it. Because they don't like this, they'll learn that it's better to stick to the lever that gives them food. The shock is so unpleasant that they'll learn to avoid it, even though the other lever gives food. Soon, they'll learn which lever to push and which lever to leave alone.

Your dog's brain works in a similar manner. When you apply some type of reinforcement to their behavior, they will learn that some behaviors are wanted, and some are not. With enough repetition, you can apply a command and see a result from your dog. Remember,

Photo Courtesy of Maria McNamara

your dog doesn't hear "Sit" and understand the meaning of the word as if they suddenly understand human language. Instead, they've figured out that you like when they put their bottom on the floor when they hear that particular sound from you.

As your dog's primary trainer, you're the one in charge of handing out reinforcements to teach your dog how to behave. Because dogs respond best with positive reinforcements, these reinforcements are known as rewards. When your dog does something good, even by accident, you need to reward them to their brain can make the connection between the action and the reward.

If you're teaching your dog a basic command, like Sit, you'll want to manipulate them into the proper position. When they hit their mark, give them some type of reward. When you give the treat, you can say something like "Good sit!" Repeat this a few times, take a break, and repeat it again. When they do what you want, make sure they are rewarded with whatever motivates them the most.

Once your dog starts to understand what is going on, add the command. Say "Sit" and move them into the position. Then reward and repeat the command:"Good sit!" This process will take a while, so make sure to practice regularly. The end goal is for your dog to hear the command and do the action without any rewards needed—it should just become second nature.

Some dog trainers will also use negative reinforcements to prevent unwanted behavior. An example of this would be to use a pronged collar or shock collar when going on walks. The rationale behind this is that the dog is doing something dangerous on walks (like chasing cars) and will correct this behavior if an unpleasant deterrent is added. When your dog does something you don't like, they'll instantly be alerted with a negative response that they'll find uncomfortable and try to avoid the behavior that warranted that response. However, this practice is controversial amongst dog trainers. If done incorrectly, this method may have a negative effect.

Primary Reinforcements

Not all reinforcements are created equally when it comes to your unique Cockapoo. Once you start to get to know your dog, you'll learn which rewards make them go wild and which ones are ignored. Primary reinforcements are rewards that are good in and of itself. These rewards have immediate value to your dog. Treats, playtime, and toys are all examples of primary reinforcement.

The best reinforcement is something that really makes your dog go nuts. For some, this is a smelly dog treat. For others, it's a favorite toy. When your reward holds your dog's attention and can make them do whatever you want, you've found the right reward.

Photo Courtesy of Louisse O'Neill

To really raise the stakes, try to find a special reward and make it scarce. If you use the same old treats or toys all the time, your Cockapoo might lose interest. You want something very special and exciting. While your dog may enjoy playing fetch with a tennis ball, is it as exciting as a stuffed animal that makes all kinds of exciting sounds? Are your training treats too similar to their usual food, or is it something extremely fragrant and tasty?

You'll find that most dogs respond to treats, but not all dogs will do tricks for just any edible thing. If your dog doesn't go for the basic treats, you'll have to find something extra special. You may go through a few different flavors before you figure out what your dog prefers. Moist training treats give off more odor than dry biscuits, so your dog might respond better to something with a little moisture in it because they can smell the reward and know what's at stake if they do a good job. Some owners even use cut up pieces of hotdogs as rewards because they're an extra special treat. Whatever you decide to use as your primary reinforcement, make sure it's exciting and always on hand.

Secondary Reinforcements

Secondary reinforcements are rewards that don't necessarily have intrinsic value but are still rewarding for a dog. You can think of secondary reinforcements as currency. On its own, paper money doesn't have any value. But we can give value to money when we trade it in for tangible items. Examples of secondary reinforcements in dog training include praise and clickers as markers of good behavior.

Because we're not made of an endless supply of dog treats, it's good to create rewards that don't always rely on food to get results. Auditory markers can let your dog know that they're doing something good without having to stop and hand over a treat. Over time, treats can pack on the pounds and can create a dent in your budget. However, this kind of training initially requires primary reinforcements to give meaning to the secondary reinforcements.

For example, a clicker is a small device that emits a sound when you push the button. When you start clicker training, give your dog a treat and a click when they do something good. Repeat the process until your dog learns that a click is meant as a reward. Then, you can give your dog just a click when they've done well, and treats can be used intermittently.

The same can be done with a voice cue. "Yes" is a common one because it's short and precise. When your dog sits, say "Yes" and give a treat. Over time, your dog will learn that your verbal cue means that they're doing a good job. That way, if you find yourself without a treat, you can reward them without giving them food.

Dangers of Negative Reinforcements

Negative reinforcements are part of operant conditioning, but you may decide that you don't want to use them with your dog. There is a thin line between self-correction and punishment, and you don't want to cross it.

Cockapoos are sensitive dogs, so they are less likely to require negative reinforcements. In fact, this kind of training may do more harm than good. Their sensitivity applies to their interactions with you. They are likely to respond to your happiness or anger. If they perceive your behavior as anger, they may become afraid of you. There are some breeds that hardly care if you're upset at them—the Cockapoo is not one of them. These little guys just want to make their owner happy, so if you do something that shows you're upset, they might get upset, too.

Photo Courtesy of
Lily House

Pain is a negative reinforcement and should not be used on dogs. This can lead to fear, which will ruin your training progress. Hitting a dog will not necessarily teach the dog to avoid bad behaviors. Instead, it will teach your dog to avoid you at all costs. If your dog is avoiding you out of fear, he is less likely to absorb your training lessons. You want your dog to be able to trust you and to feel safe around you. Once you go too far with negative reinforcements, you give your dog a reason not to trust you at all.

Hiring a Trainer and Attending Classes

Hiring a trainer or going to classes is absolutely beneficial for training your dog. Even if you have a general idea of how to train a dog, an expert can really boost your training practice. You may come across issues that you don't know how to resolve but your trainer has encountered many times before. Chances are that you've probably only ever worked with a few dogs in your life. Trainers, on the other hand, work with multiple dogs every day. They have the experience to help you with any problem that pops up along the way. They're also great at reassuring you when you're feeling stressed about your dog's behavior.

Group classes are also great for helping your dog socialize with others. Your dog doesn't necessarily have to get too close to the other dogs during class, but they'll have to relax enough to learn with lots of canine distractions around them. As you'll find when you work with your dog, it's one thing to train without distractions and another to train in a strange place with lots of people and dogs around.

There are many trainers to choose from, and all of them have slightly different ideas about the best way to train a dog. Some are good, while others will not be the right fit for you and your dog. If you're completely lost on where to start, talk to a fellow dog owner and ask for recommendations. You'll want someone who believes in positive training practices and is widely recommended by others. You're essentially trusting this person to do what's best for your dog, so you want the right trainer for the job. If the trainer is too focused on strange tactics and is very stern with dogs, they might be too harsh for a Cockapoo. But if the trainer uses positive-only or very gentle corrections, they're probably best suited to work with you as you train your dog.

Owner Behavior

Don't forget, your dog is constantly watching you and trying to make sense of your reactions to their behavior. They will soon understand when you're happy and when you're angry. This breed loves to see you happy. They're companion animals and will want to be by your side at all times. If you're angry with them while you train because you're frustrated by their behavior, they're not going to want to train anymore. However, when you're dealing with a little creature with a mind of its own, you're inevitably going to become frustrated.

To combat this frustration, remember that your dog is not a tiny human. They do not learn and understand things in the same way we do. To us, it's obvious that unwanted behaviors can be harmful. To a dog, they're just acting out of instinct and will continue to do so until they learn otherwise.

Also, remember that training doesn't happen overnight. If you work on a command for a day and your Cockapoo just isn't getting it, that's perfectly normal. You may have to practice the same command every day for months before they can do it on cue. Don't give up because things seem difficult. Instead, ask for some assistance from an expert and keep practicing.

If you can't hide your disappointment or frustration, take a break. It's not worth it to get so worked up that you end up lashing out at your dog. When you feel your emotions getting out of control, take a step back with the intention of picking things back up when everyone has had the chance to cool down. Training is important, but not as important as the close bond between you and your Cockapoo.

Dog training is no easy task. It takes knowledge, practice, and a good mindset. Especially if you're new to dog ownership, it takes a while to think like a dog. They've got their own ideas and quirks that are completely foreign to humans. But once you figure out what motivates them, you're on your way to having a well-trained dog. When training, be persistent, calm, and positive, and your Cockapoo will enjoy this time you spend together.

CHAPTER 11
Dealing with Unwanted Behaviors

"Cockapoos can nip at first, which is what they do with their litter-mates, and which can be perceived as biting. It might also be caused by teething. Channel the behavior. If they perceive long periods of "isolation" (not at night of course), they can view that as separation, which can lead to anxiety. Be consistent."

Jeanne Davis
Windhorse Offering

Everyone wants a well-behaved dog. When you're at home relaxing, you want your dog to be calm and cuddly. When you want to have some fun with your dog, you'll want them to play with you and go on walks. When you go in public, you want your dog to be friendly and listen to you. And at every time in between, you want your dog to behave himself and not destroy everything you own. Unfortunately, no dog is perfect, and you'll eventually run into issues with your dog's behavior. This chapter should help you start troubleshooting your dog's naughty or confusing behavior and figure out a plan to combat it.

What is Bad Behavior in Dogs?

It's hard to create a precise definition of bad behavior because it's largely relative to an owner's preference. One owner may be fine with their dog barking at all hours of the day, while others cannot tolerate it. As an owner, you must decide how you want your dog to behave, and then take the steps to ensure that behavior is taught.

A lot of bad behavior boils down to annoying habits, destructive tendencies, and dangerous behavior. There can be quite the range of behaviors, but even the smallest bad behavior can create discord in your home.

Annoying behaviors are those that aren't necessarily going to do any serious harm but are not polite behaviors. Barking, jumping on people, and crowding the front door are a few actions that drive dog owners insane. If your dog barks every time someone walks by your house, it's not really going

Photo Courtesy of Sue Walters

to hurt anyone. If it happens once, it's not even that big of a deal. But when it happens constantly, that's where the behavior becomes a problem. Left unchecked, your dog could be barking for hours every day. You'll never be able to make a quiet phone call or sleep through the entire night. If you live in an apartment, you're disturbing everyone else who lives in your building. It can be a serious problem if it isn't caught immediately and dealt with in the right way.

Destructive behaviors ruin your property and make it impossible to leave your dog unsupervised. We all have busy lives that require us to leave the house sometimes. If your dog insists on digging, chewing, and peeing on everything you own, you're going to have problems when you can't go to the grocery store without returning to destruction. If things get bad enough, you might wonder if you can even continue to care for your dog, especially if you live in rented property.

Finally, some owners have issues with aggressive dogs that threaten humans and other animals. This is by far the most serious of the bad behaviors. You might have a mischievous dog with a high prey drive that wants to hunt your cats. Or you may have a dog that plays too rough at the dog park and tries to fight other dogs. Or your dog may be great with you but bites at other people who want to pet him. In any case, these behaviors can cause a dog to be surrendered to a shelter or worse. Other behaviors may be handled by the owner with time, but any situation in which another living being is at risk by your dog, immediate, professional help is necessary.

91

Finding the Root of the Problem

Your dog doesn't misbehave because they are a bad dog. There are many reasons why dogs do the things that they do. It's your job to think like a dog and figure out their motivations.

Sometimes, your dog is just acting upon natural instincts. If your Cockapoo is chasing after smaller animals, it's probably because Poodles were originally bred to hunt rats and they're just trying to do their job. Or, maybe they're digging in your yard because it's hot outside and the burrow they're creating is helping them stay cool. Or your puppy is gnawing on your table legs because they're teething and their gums hurt. Before you scold your dog, make sure all of their canine needs are being met. There's a chance that they're doing something annoying because it's in their nature to do it.

Another reason dogs are naughty is because they're bored. Especially in intelligent breeds like the Cockapoo, dogs act out because they aren't getting enough entertainment or mental stimulation. These dogs love to play and be challenged. If no one is around to play with them, they might create their own games. These fun activities can include digging, chewing, and destroying anything within reach. If you have to be away from your dog for an extended period of time, try to make sure their needs are attended to before you leave. If possible, give them a puzzle toy before you leave the house to give them some entertainment while you're away. If that's not enough for your active Cockapoo, consider taking your dog to a doggy daycare or hiring a dog walker to spend a little time with your pup. It can be expensive, but not as expensive as replacing all of your furniture.

Or your dog might be destructive because he has separation anxiety. As mentioned in earlier chapters, some sensitive dogs suffer from separation anxiety to the point that they potty in the house or destroy your belongings. If your dog makes a mess when you're not home, this might be the root of the problem. If other methods of entertaining your pooch don't work, your veterinarian may be able to suggest supplements or medications that can help your dog relax.

If your dog is aggressive, make sure that they're not afraid of other people or animals. It sounds counterintuitive, but fear is what causes a lot of animals to lash out and harm others. One way to combat this aggression is to slowly socialize your dog with others. Do whatever you can to make your dog feel more comfortable around others, to the point where people or dogs can get near your dog without them showing any signs of aggression. In the meantime, make sure your dog doesn't get too close to anyone. You will have to be under constant supervision of your dog until you can trust him to behave. In the meantime, seek help from a professional dog behavioralist to nip the dangerous behaviors in the bud.

Bad Behavior Prevention

There are a few things you can do to prevent the generalized naughty behavior. For starters, make sure you're giving your dog enough physical and mental exercise. A tired dog is a good dog, so you'll want to keep your dog active so they don't have the extra energy to be bad. Try increasing the amount of daily exercise by at least a half hour. Take longer walks, try to move a little faster, and choose strenuous games to play in between walks.

Photo Courtesy of Julie Nicklin

Also, work on your training skills. Sometimes, it just takes your dog a little practice to get into "work mode". When you've been working really hard on your commands, your dog may feel as though they have a new responsibility to behave. The extra attention and activity may be enough to keep your dog out of trouble. Similarly, group classes are filled with different sights and sounds, so an hour walking around the ring might keep your dog calm for the rest of the night.

Finally, try to maintain some consistency with your dog. If you correct your dog when they bark on some occasions, make sure you aren't lenient at other times when you don't feel like training. Every time your dog misbehaves is a learning opportunity. Correct bad behavior, then praise good behavior. Don't forget that positive reinforcement goes a long way, even when your dog is doing something wrong.

How to Properly Correct Your Dog

Photo Courtesy of Jackie Massa

Correcting your dog is different from punishment. The goal is to catch unwanted behaviors and redirect their attention towards something more acceptable. Then, once your dog's behavior has changed, you need to reinforce the good behavior. This way, you can teach your dog how to behave within the context of their natural instincts or desires.

For example, let's say that your Cockapoo runs to the front door and barks incessantly at the sound of the doorbell. This is annoying behavior that may make the visitor fearful of your dog. Naturally, you're going to want to keep them from barking, but yelling at them doesn't seem to help. In fact, it only makes them bark more.

Instead of barking back at your dog, do something to catch their attention. A loud clap, a can of rocks, or a stern "no" should hopefully be enough to confuse them for a split second. In that time, give your dog a command. "On your bed" is a good one for this situation, but a "sit" or "down" will also suffice. Do something that will reroute their mind and give them a job to do. If they can accomplish this task with your help, give them lots of treats and love. You can practice this every time someone comes to the door. With enough work, you should get to the point where your dog hears the doorbell and automatically lies on their bed, without the use of rewards.

Of course, this is all easier said than done. It takes a lot of hard work to change your dog's behaviors. That's why it's so important to properly socialize and train your puppy from the start so you can remove the opportunity to pick up bad habits. However, if you're adopting a dog that's already had time to pick up bad habits, then you might spend half of your training time correcting these quirks.

When to Call a Professional

Sometimes, we just don't have the experience or expertise to deal with the issue. Your dog's problematic behavior might get to the point where you just don't know what to do anymore. When you're at the end of your rope, find a helpful resource. A trainer, vet, or breeder may be able to point you in the right direction. Otherwise, the behavior will spiral out of control to where you might not be able to keep your dog in your home. Of course, if your dog is a danger to others, you need immediate help. Some dog trainers will even come to your home so you don't have to worry about bringing your problem dog into public spaces. No matter how minuscule or insignificant the bad behavior seems, it's always worth it to work on positive ways to correct the behavior because it will make your relationship with your dog so much better!

It can be extremely frustrating if your dog is annoying, destructive, or downright dangerous. Everyone wants their dog to be a perfect canine citizen. However, good behavior takes a lot of work. Dogs aren't naturally polite. They like to make their own rules when they can get away with it. It's your job as an owner to keep an eye on your dog and stop bad behaviors before they become habits. It can be difficult to go against their strange ideas, but there are tons of resources to help you along the way.

CHAPTER 12
Basic Commands

"Cockapoos are usually pretty easy to train. I suggest that new owners find a basic puppy obedience class once the puppy is protected by the usual puppy vaccinations. The owners can benefit learning training techniques at the basic obedience class. It will enhance the experience of raising a puppy."

Linda S. Oberling
Cockapoos by Choice

Cockapoos are amazing, intelligent dogs that can do so many cool things. When you work hard on training, there's no limit to what your dog can learn. When you're just starting out with your new dog, it's good to master a few basics before moving on to the fun tricks. This chapter will cover a few of the most important basic commands to teach your dog and give a few tips and tricks to help you along the way.

Benefits of Proper Training

There are so many reasons to obedience train your dog. Well-trained dogs are generally safer, politer, and less hyperactive than dogs that are left to their own devices. Training is a good way to keep your dog's mind active, keeping them from getting bored and making trouble. Good obedience training can save your dog's life in certain situations.

For example, imagine a scenario where your dog gets loose and you need to get them back by your side before they get lost or hit by a car. In this situation, you want to be able to call their name and give the Come command to recall them. Then, you'll want them to sit or lie by your side until you can grab their collar or put their leash back on. But if your dog doesn't know any of these commands, they'll continue to wander around, making it difficult to retrieve them. Hopefully you'll never have to be in a scary situation with your dog, but good training could make a huge difference in your dog's safety.

In general, obedience training makes your dog much more pleasant to be around. Once you start working on commands, you'll find all sorts of practical applications for them. And all of these basic commands are prerequisites for more difficult commands. Once you master a few, you can start working on more challenging tricks.

*Photo Courtesy of
Sarah Spursettes*

Places to Practice

Photo Courtesy of Diana Gregory

Starting out, you'll probably practice your commands at your house. The home is a good place to begin your practice because it's familiar and you can control the number of distractions around. A room with plenty of space to move is a good starting spot. That way, your dog's attention is on you and the awesome rewards you have to offer.

However, you'll want to move outside the home at some point. You want your commands to have practical, real-world applications, so you need your dog to be able to respond in unfamiliar places.

For example, your dog may be awesome at sitting when you're at home. In fact, you might not even need to bribe your Cockapoo with treats when you want them to sit. But perhaps you go for a walk in a new park and need your dog to sit for a second while you take a phone call or tie your shoe. If your dog has never needed to sit in a place with tons of distractions, they may not obey the first few times. For this reason, it's important to create some variation in location when you train.

Start off slow and work your way up to more challenging locations. Begin inside your home, then move to a familiar spot outside, like the backyard. Then, practice in familiar parks or at a friend's house. Finally, try to do a few commands at a farmer's market or somewhere unfamiliar with a ton of distractions. When your dog can obey you under slight stress, then you know that they've got the command down.

Clicker Training

As mentioned in the previous chapter, some trainers like to use clickers or verbal markers in conjunction with treats. This requires you to "click" or make an affirmative sound, like "Yes" every time your dog does the right thing. This allows for greater accuracy when rewarding your dog, it doesn't require you to carry treats everywhere you go, and you don't need to feed your dog as many rewards as you might if you didn't use a clicker.

When starting out with clicker training, use a click and a treat at once. This way, your dog connects the action with the reward and the sound. Use both the clicker and the treat for a while to make sure the connection is made. Eventually, you'll be able to use your clicker as a reward instead of a treat.

The reason this is more accurate than handing out treats is because the sound of the clicker is instantaneous. The second your dog's bottom touches the floor, you can give a click. When you're dealing with treats, you have to watch and wait for your dog to settle into the command before handing the treat over. If you're working on multiple commands at once, it's not easy to stop your progress to reward your dog. With a clicker, you can hand out as many rewards as you want with precision.

Another reason it's accurate is because your Cockapoo won't do the commands perfectly the first time. If you're using treats, you may accidentally give your dog the treat at the wrong time and reinforce the wrong action. A clicker can show your dog that they're on the right track with reinforcing the right movement. For example, maybe you're teaching your dog to roll over. To do this, you must first teach your dog the Down command. With clicker training, you might give your dog a click for hitting the down movement, even if he doesn't make the full roll. With this method, your dog understands that "Down" is an important part of the "Roll over" process, even if he hasn't figured out the whole command quite yet.

One downfall of the clicker method is that you always need your clicker on hand for training. For some owners, this isn't an issue. For others, it can be hard to remember to bring the little device wherever you go. For this reason, you may choose to use a verbal cue like "Yes" or "Good" or whatever affirmative noise you can think of that will let your dog know they are doing what you want them to do. However, once you pick a noise, stick to it. Otherwise, you're going to create confusion.

Basic Commands

There are so many commands to teach your Cockapoo, but some are definitely more important than others. There will be lots of time to work on fun tricks later, so stick to the basic commands to start. The following five commands are the building blocks on which you will obedience train your dog. Once you master all five, you'll find that life with your dog is so much easier because you finally have a little control over their wacky ideas. Once you master these commands, continue practicing them throughout your dog's life and build upon their knowledge with more advanced commands.

Sit

This is perhaps the first command you'll teach your dog because it's easy for Cockapoos to do and it's easy to teach. This command can be used in so many different scenarios. When you need your dog to wait or calm down for a moment, Sit is a good command to keep them quiet and still.

To teach this command, you'll want your dog in a standing position. Hold a treat in your hand and move it above and slightly past their nose. They should follow the treat with their nose, naturally causing them to sit. If this doesn't work, you can gently place your hand on their bottom and apply light pressure to show them what you want them to do. Once they are in the sitting position, give them a treat and lots of praise. After you've got the motion down, start adding the command "Sit" before they sit. When they do this command, the implication is that they will remain seated until you give them further commands, or release them by saying, "Okay."

Down

Once you teach Sit, you'll want to try Down. This is a bit trickier than the Sit command because your dog might not naturally want to lie on the ground on command. But it's useful for times where you want your dog to chill out for a little longer than you might put them in a sit. It also takes them a little bit longer to spring into action from a Down position, so when it's paired with a Stay it will give them more time to chill out.

To teach this, start with your dog in the Sit position. Hold the treat in front of their nose, then slowly move it towards the floor. They will follow the treat with their nose, but when it gets too close to the ground, they will naturally lower their body. You want your dog to go all the way to the floor. If they only go part way down, it's easy for them to spring back up. Once they are on the ground, give them their treat and praise.

If they have a hard time following the reward, you can try to gently nudge them into position with their leash. Try not to tug or force them down. Instead, gently apply downward pressure to the leash while moving the treat in front of their face to show them how to get into the Down position. Once you have them where you want them, give them treats and praise.

Photo Courtesy of Christine Kirby

Stay

This command can be tricky to teach, especially if you have an active puppy with a short attention span. However, it can come in handy if your pup loves to roam around and get into trouble. The Stay command is useful because when it's done right, your dog will freeze in place until they're given further instructions. If you find yourself in a situation where you need to leave your dog for a moment and don't want them to follow you, this command will be extremely useful.

To teach this, start with your dog in the Sit position. This gives them the hint that they're supposed to be performing a certain action. Place your hand in front of their face like a stop sign and say "Stay." Walk back a few steps while holding out your palm, pause a moment, then return. If they're still motionless when you return, give them their reward. If they break, put them back into a Sit and Stay and try again.

When you're starting out, don't take more than a few steps away. Naturally, they're going to want to follow you. Over time, build up the distance between you and your pup. You can also add challenging variables, like turning your back towards your dog, leaving the room, and even circling them. When you want to practice long distances in distracting environments, buy a 20-foot leash to give your dog some extra distance while still maintaining some control over them.

If your dog has a tough time staying still, practice this command on a leash. That way, you can drop the leash and put a foot on it when they start to get up. This should "self-correct" and make it harder for them to move. Or you might even want to start slower by putting them in a Stay and simply moving from their side to in front of them. Then, once they can stay still, face them and walk backward. At first, your Cockapoo will want to follow you and stay by your side. Over time, they'll understand that you're going to return and relax a little.

Come

Being able to recall your dog is so important. Occasionally, your dog will be doing something they shouldn't be doing, and you will need a way to get them close to your side. Or you may encounter a dangerous situation and you need to protect your dog or keep them out of the way. If your Cockapoo likes to wander, the Come command can save their life.

To teach this, put your dog in a Sit and Stay. When you're a few feet away, call your dog towards you. If you have a treat in your hand, your Cockapoo will likely hear your enthusiastic voice, see your open arms, and come barreling towards you. When your dog comes to you, put a hand on their collar so they don't run away and give them a treat.

If they don't run straight towards you, try nudging them along with the leash. When your dog is in the Sit and Stay, take the leash with you and call your dog. If they don't immediately come to you, give a gentle tug. This should redirect their attention to you, prompting them to approach you. Then, they'll be more inclined to come to you if you are waiting for them with treats and praise.

Because you want your dog to come to you every time, avoid calling them if you're only going to yell at them. Our dogs do things that frustrate us, but the Come command should not be used to call your dog for punishment. If your dog learns that responding to "Come" is not always a positive experience, they will not want to do it. If they have an unreliable recall, they may not respond to you when it really counts. For this reason, if your dog comes to you, make sure you give them tons of affection and praise so they will continue to do so.

Leash Training

Cockapoos love to go on walks with their humans. It's a great way to exercise while spending quality time together. However, if your dog doesn't walk very well on a leash, walks will become a tedious chore that will leave you frustrated. From the first moment you clip the leash onto your dog's collar, it's time to start practicing good walking habits. The more you leash train with your dog in the early days, the happier you'll be in the long run. It's not natural for dogs to walk right next to you on a leash, especially if they're curious and love to explore. Lots of quality practice is necessary for teaching your dog how to act polite on walks.

To start, your dog should be positioned on your left side. They should walk in line with you, not too far ahead nor lagging behind. There should not be any tension in the leash; it should hang loosely between you. When you stop, your dog should stop and sit by your side. When you turn, your dog should turn along with you, speeding up or slowing down to remain in position at your left side. Easier said than done, right?

It takes a ton of practice to get your dog to walk nicely. Sometimes, you'll feel like you're flying a kite because of the way your dog moves erratically around you. It's easy to give up on training and let your dog take control while he gets his exercise, but this behavior will get old very quickly. Good leash training will keep your dog in check and make walks much more pleasant.

Before you go on your walk, get your dog to sit on your left side. This is a nice way to say, "I'm in charge here, and we're going to do

Photo Courtesy of Michael Hibberd

things my way." Hold the end of the leash with your right hand and slide your left hand down your leash to keep your dog close. Also, keep a lot of treats on hand because you'll need to give out rewards every time your dog walks nicely.

Say, "Let's go" and take a few steps forward. If they walk alongside you without pulling, give them tons of praise and a treat. It helps to talk to your dog while you walk so that their focus is on you and not all the distractions around them. Tell them about how good they're being. If they start to pull or get distracted, give a quick tug on the leash to remind them what they need to do. Don't yank too hard or drag your dog. Instead, a quick pop will help keep them in line without hurting them. When there is slack on the leash again, praise and reward them.

Along with walking, practice changing your pace. Slow down and direct your dog to do the same. Or you can speed up and get your dog really moving. Work on right turns, left turns, and about-faces. Halt suddenly and have your dog sit beside you. Instruct your dog to wait at crosswalks or just in the middle of the sidewalk while you tie your shoe. Incorporate different events into your walk to practice real-life scenarios that may come up on your walk. All the while, your dog's shoulders should be in line (or very close) with your leg.

Sometimes, dogs have a really hard time walking on a leash. Pulling is a serious issue that can make walks a chore. If your dog is difficult, there are different harnesses and collars to try. If you choose a harness, pick one with the leash fastener on the front. This way, your dog is unable to pull without spinning them towards you. Avoid harnesses that clip on from the back, because this only makes it more comfortable for them to drag you down the street. Some trainers use pronged collars for serious cases because it allows your dog to self-correct without injuring themselves. However, it's important to use positive training alongside any kind of self-correction methods. Choke chains can injure a dog's throat if they pull too hard and should be avoided. Ideally, the flat collar should be used on all dogs, but sometimes other measures need to be taken to keep you and your dog safe on a walk. If you have serious issues with walks, talk to a trainer to help you with your difficult pooch.

When going on walks, remember to give frequent feedback to your dog. Let them know when they're doing a good job, and correct them when they're not doing so well. Bring lots of treats (and maybe some water) when you go on your daily walks to encourage your dog to explore new places and be on their best behavior. With lots of hard work, you'll love the special time of day when you and your buddy get to enjoy some time in nature together.

Once you master the basic commands, keep practicing! Even better, keep building upon their knowledge with new commands. When you get busy or have a hard time training, it's easy to give up and forget about obedience training. However, it's best to start good habits at an early age. That way, your dog doesn't have the time to make their own rules. Stick with it and remember that there are lots of experts out there who can help you train your dog to be the best Cockapoo ever!

CHAPTER 13
Advanced Commands

Once you have mastered the basic commands, it's time to move onto something a little more challenging! Some of these commands are very useful when it comes to having a safe and polite dog. Other commands serve no real purpose other than to have fun. There are countless commands to teach your Cockapoo, but here are a few that you might want to try with your furry friend.

Leave It

This command will come in handy with your curious pup. Your Cockapoo will want to stick their nose into anything that looks interesting. While it's nice to allow your dog to explore the world around you, sometimes you just know what's best for them. This command is useful if they are focused on something they shouldn't be, like a squirrel they want to chase or a dead animal they want to roll in.

To teach this, find a treat they'll really want. Set it on the ground with your foot nearby. Naturally, they're going to approach the treat so they can eat it. When they get close, cover the treat with your foot so it's unavailable. Show them that they can't just eat any treat on the ground.

Try it again, asking them to leave it. If they make a bee-line for the treat, tell them "No" and cover the treat. Repeat this until they appear uninterested or wait for the treat. If they successfully leave the treat, mark the behavior with a "Yes" and give them the treat. This command should teach them to break their concentration when you tell them to "Leave it." When your dog starts to get the hang of this command, you can command your dog to "Leave it," then teach them to "Take it."

Drop It

Drop It is another command that can save your dog's life. Dogs will put anything in their mouth. Sometimes, the things they find are easy to choke on or will make them sick. This command will ensure that if you catch them with something they shouldn't have, they'll drop it instantly.

This command can be taught during playtime. Throw a ball and have them fetch it. If your dog doesn't automatically hand it over, this is the time to teach the skill. Show your dog that you have a treat. They'll want to eat it but can't because there's already a ball in their mouth. If the treat is more rewarding than the ball, they'll drop the ball in favor of the treat. When they do this, say "Good drop it!" and praise them. After a few tries, start using the command when they come to you with the ball. If they drop it when you ask, give them the treat and praise, then throw the ball again for an added reward. Once your dog has the hang of this, move on to different objects until they drop everything on command.

Photo Courtesy of
Liam Thompson

Look at Me

Photo Courtesy of Joyce Wilson

This command is good for getting your dog to focus on you. This is extremely useful when you're going on walks because you want your dog to follow your lead. It's also useful when you want to break your dog's attention on something else, like a car they'd like to chase. Let's not forget that this is also a useful skill when you'd like your dog to look at the camera for an adorable photo.

Start with your dog in the sitting position. Hold a treat in each hand, close to their nose so they know what's at stake. Then, say, "Look at me" while slowly drawing both hands towards your nose. Naturally, their eyes will follow the treat and they'll look right at you. If they hold the gaze for even just a second, bring both hands forward, but only release one treat. The reason you want to use both hands is that it gets your dog to look at the center of your face, and not just follow one hand to the treat.

When your dog figures this out, try the command without leading your dog's gaze to your face with the treat. Instead, maybe just point at your nose for a hint. Then, give your dog the treats and praise. Eventually, you'll get to the point where your dog will stare at you when you give the command.

Shake

Shake is a fairly simple trick to teach that's fun to show off. Start by facing your dog in the sitting position. Hold a treat in your hand and place it where you would meet their paw if you were about to shake. For some dogs, this will cause them to put their paw on your hand in an attempt to knock the treat from your hand. If this happens, give them your hand and give their paw a shake. Afterward, give them the treat and lots of praise.

If this method doesn't work, you can always nudge your dog in the right direction by picking up their paw and putting it into the position you want. Add the verbal cue and reward, and your dog will be shaking on command in no time.

108

Sit Pretty

This command is all about the cute factor. Along with this trick being absolutely adorable, it will help with your dog's core strength, if that kind of thing is important to you. If your dog hasn't used these muscles a lot, then it's going to take some time to get used to sitting like a person. Your dog will probably be a little wobbly at first. Keep practicing until they can hold the position.

To teach this command, have your dog start in the sitting position. Hold a treat in front of their nose, then slowly move it up and back behind their head. If they're following the treat with their nose, they'll naturally lift their body so they don't tip over. Reward them if they lift off of their front paws. Keep practicing until your dog can sit on their hind legs with their paws in front of their belly.

Roll Over/Play Dead

Especially when paired with fun hand actions and sound effects, Play Dead is a crowd-pleaser of a trick. Be forewarned, if your dog does not like to expose their belly to people, this is going to be a challenge. It's not natural for every dog to feel comfortable in that position.

Start with a sitting dog. Use the treat to guide your dog into the following positions. Lower the treat to the floor to get them lying down. Then, slowly rotate the treat around their head, until they lie on their side. Praise them and give the reward if your dog hits the desired "dead" position. Some owners like to make a gun with their hand and say "Bang!" as the command word. Others like to say "Dead dog" or "Play dead." Your dog will respond to whatever cues you teach him, so feel free to get creative.

A Play Dead is halfway to a Roll Over. Instead of stopping the rolling motion when your dog gets to their side, continue rotating the treat for an entire roll. It may take some time until your dog is able to make a full revolution. But when he does, make sure to give your dog a ton of praise because it's a fairly challenging trick.

Crawl

Photo Courtesy of Susie Thomas

This is another fun trick that's easy to teach if your dog already knows basic commands. You'll have so much fun watching your dog wiggle around on the ground.

To teach this command, start with your dog in the down position. Hold the treat between their paws, then slowly move it towards you. If you move the treat too quickly, your dog will probably pop back up to standing. As your dog moves towards you, you'll have to back up a little so there's enough room for your dog to move. If your dog crawls a foot or two, give them their reward. Keep practicing while increasing the distance, and then try getting them to crawl without the use of the treat.

Competitions for Cockapoos

If you find that your Cockapoo really enjoys obedience training and performing tricks, there are fun competitions out there where your dog can show off their skills. Your dog doesn't need to be a champion to be able to participate in such events. Consider joining a local dog club to get training help and information about events in your area.

Obedience competitions are a fun way to test your dog's ability and your training skills. These competitions will take you and your dog through a series of challenges. Your dog will be expected to walk nicely on a leash and to sit and stay with a bunch of other dogs around him. Some dogs really love to get into the ring and strut their stuff, so if your dog is great at obedience training, it might be a fun activity for the two of you.

Nose work is another fun class you can take that can lead to competitions. This activity is kind of like drug or explosive sniffing, but without the drugs or explosives! Instead, you'll use little containers with essential oil scents to teach your dog how to sniff out and identify different con-

tainers. This is a great way to burn some mental energy, especially when the weather doesn't permit you to spend a lot of time outside.

Agility competitions can also be a lot of fun for a Cockapoo. Competitions are divided into classes based on dog size, so your little dog won't have to go up against a big, fast dog. The easily trained and energetic Cockapoo can do well in this event because it requires them to follow their owner's direction and race through a series of obstacles. It might take a few classes for your dog to figure out how to do the activity, but once your Cockapoo has aced the course, you can compete against other dogs and owners to complete the course the fastest and take home the prize.

If you can master these advanced commands with no problem, then don't stop here! Once you've figured out the basics of how to teach commands, you can use your creativity to come up with cool tricks that you won't find in the competition ring. You might be able to teach your Cockapoo how to open doors or even fetch a drink from the fridge. When it comes to positive reinforcement, you can teach your dog just about anything!

CHAPTER 14
Traveling with Cockapoos

"Most Cockapoos travel very well. There are exceptions and a few may get motion sickness. However, I often hear reports that the owners take them camping, fishing, beach walking, trail walking, swimming, etc."

Linda S. Oberling
Cockapoos by Choice

There's going to be a day where you'll need to leave home with your Cockapoo. Whether you're moving halfway across the country or just visiting the vet, your dog will need to be transported away from their familiar home. For some dogs, this can be a very stressful time. For others, it's a ton of fun. The difference is mostly in preparation and your attitude towards traveling with your pup. This chapter will cover some information that will hopefully make your dog happy and safe when it comes to going on adventures with you!

Photo Courtesy of
Angela McCartney Prentice

*Photo Courtesy of
Nicola Welch*

Dog Carriers and Restraints

If you insist that your car passengers wear seatbelts, then your dog should be no exception. In the event of a car crash, your dog will become a projectile and can become seriously injured. It doesn't take a lot of speed or impact for your dog to be launched forward or knocked off balance. You would be absolutely devastated if your dog was injured when many auto accident injuries are preventable.

Similarly, if you wanted to transport your furry passenger safely, you would try to minimize any distractions that would impair your driving. This includes said furry passenger running all over the car, or even hopping onto your lap. It doesn't take a lot of activity to momentarily become distracted and disaster can strike quickly. Your dog should be in the backseat and unable to move freely around the car.

This is why safety restraints are so important for dogs. There are many different types of products on the market, so it's not hard to find one to suit your dog's needs.

If you are crate training, the crate can keep your dog safe and secure in case of a crash. When secured in your car, the crate keeps your dog from being thrown around in a crash. Plus, it adds another layer of protection to keep your dog safe from flying debris. If you have one of the smaller varieties of Cockapoo, there are soft traveling cases to transport your dog in. These are often used for air travel and can keep your dog contained in the event of a crash. The soft sides of the carrier aren't as resistant to impact, but it can keep your dog safer than if they were not restrained at all.

There are also seatbelts available for dogs that don't like to be in tight spaces. These are affordable safety belts that can be attached to a dog's collar and buckled into a car's existing seatbelts. When using these, you may choose to put your dog in a harness, then attach the seatbelt to the harness clip. Otherwise, a car crash may cause neck injury if your dog is restrained by the collar around their neck. With a harness, your dog will be pulled around their shoulders, reducing trauma to the head and neck.

Whichever method you choose, it's important to regularly use some form of restraint to keep your dog safe. It will give you some peace of mind to know that your Cockapoo is a little bit safer in your car. Plus, all of your passengers are safer when your dog isn't able to run amok in the car!

Photo Courtesy of Harriet Draper

Photo Courtesy of
@cockapoograham on Instagram

Preparing Your Dog for Car Rides

Sometimes dogs get nervous in the car. When you look at it from their perspective, it makes sense. You're asking your dog to jump into a strange box that moves very fast. There are so many strange sights and sensations that it can be downright overwhelming. Some dogs love nothing more than to ride in a car, but for other dogs, car rides are a great source of anxiety. This anxiety can also lead to car sickness, which will make your dog absolutely miserable. The best way to make your dog enjoy car rides is to slowly prepare them for your vehicle.

To start, let your dog explore your car while it's in park. Let your dog sniff around the back seat and give them treats if they're staying calm. You might even shut the door and take your place in the driver's seat as if you were going on a drive. Then, try out your dog's restraint and reward them if they can handle being restrained in the car.

Next, it's time to start driving. Take short drives around the block, talking to your dog in a soothing voice and praising them for staying calm. Give your dog a reward before getting out of the car. Increase the time spent in the car, gradually increasing the drive duration until your dog is no longer fearful.

For extreme cases of car-related anxiety and car sickness, talk to your vet about other things you can do to help your dog. For situational anxiety, a vet may decide to prescribe medication to give your dog in the event that they need to be in the car.

Not every dog will have this aversion to the car. You may find that your Cockapoo puppy jumps into your car with no problem and never wants to leave. But if your dog is nervous in your car, you'll want to address this fear before it becomes necessary to transport your dog somewhere.

If you're going on a long car trip, make sure to take frequent stops. While humans can go for hours without needing to stop, your dog will get antsy if they're cooped up for too long. Find rest stops along the way that have plenty of space for your dog to stretch their legs. Also, make sure that water is readily available for your thirsty pooch. Try making a stop in a city with a dog park, if possible. Being able to let your dog play freely in a safe place will make them so much happier than if they're only allowed a quick potty break at an interstate rest stop.

Flying and Hotel Stays

Sometimes the adventures you go on with your pooch require air travel or hotel stays. A completely new environment can confuse your dog, so you definitely need to take some extra precautions. The first thing you need to decide is if it's worth the hassle to take such a long trip with your dog. If you're making a big move or there's no one to watch your dog, then airplanes and hotel stays may be unavoidable. But if you think your travels will stress you and your dog too much, then you might decide to leave your Cockapoo at home with a trusted person.

Air travel can be especially stressful for a dog. For this reason, it's best if you only fly in extreme circumstances. Unfortunately, it's too common that an airline loses precious cargo or a dog suffers a medical emergency in the air. If you're not willing to deal with that risk, it might be better to drive.

If that's just not possible, there are some things you can do to ease your mind while flying with your dog. If you have a small Cockapoo that can fit in an airline-approved carrier, find an airline that allows small dogs in the cabin. You won't necessarily be able to have your dog on your lap, but it will make both you and your dog feel better to be close.

If your Cockapoo is too big for the cabin, they'll have to ride in the cargo hold in a crate. Make sure they have plenty of access to water because the high altitude can be dehydrating. Make sure their crate is com-

Photo Courtesy of
Diana Gregory

fortable and maybe throw in a familiar toy to ease their worries. The cargo area can be loud and frightening to a dog, so talk to your vet to see if there's anything you can give your dog to keep them calm on the flight. It's a good idea to take your dog to the vet for a checkup before a flight to make sure they're in good health before putting them in a potentially dangerous situation.

You'll also want to take special care to ensure that your dog cannot be lost. Before your trip, look up important phone numbers for your airline and save them in your cell phone. Put a tag or label on your dog's crate with all of your contact information. Make sure you know where you need to be to pick up your dog and who to contact if there are issues.

Once you get to your destination, you'll have to stay in an unfamiliar place. When booking a hotel, make sure they allow pets and you pay whatever deposit is needed. Even the most well-behaved dog will leave behind traces and you don't want to face heavy fines for breaking the rules. Also, try to find a hotel that is located somewhere you can walk your Cockapoo. If you find yourself surrounded by cement, it might take some extra effort to find a spot to let your dog use the bathroom. Also, lots of exercise can make your stay more enjoyable. If your dog isn't bouncing off the walls or nervously destructive, then you'll be much more likely to have a good time.

If you can, try to bring some familiar items to make your dog feel more at home. A favorite blanket and a few toys can make your dog feel more at ease.

Kenneling vs. Dog Sitters

Sometimes it's just not worth it to take your dog on a trip with you. If you're flying, going on a long drive, or too busy to spend lots of quality time with your dog in a strange place, it might be best to leave them at home. When you leave your dog with a trusted person, your choices are to board your dog in a kennel or hire a dog sitter to visit your dog in your home. Both options have their pros and cons, so it's best to decide based on what is best for you and your dog.

A good doggy daycare will keep your pooch supervised and entertained all day. These boarding facilities have a small kennel for your dog to sleep in alone but also allow for your dog to play with others. These facilities keep people on staff to tend to your dog's needs at any time throughout the day (as well as overnight). You'll feel at peace to know that if something goes wrong with your dog, there will be someone

Photo Courtesy of David Thomas

around to check in on your pup. During the day, your dog will never be bored with the endless playtime with other dogs.

However, this set up isn't best for all dogs. If your dog is especially submissive around other dogs or has had issues with other dogs in the past, you might not feel comfortable leaving your dog to play with others without your supervision. It's more expensive to hire one person to take care of your dog, but it might be worth it if your dog becomes stressed around other dogs.

Look for a pet sitter who can make frequent visits to your house. You want to maintain your dog's normal schedule if possible. Make sure your sitter can stop by briefly to let your dog out and hang around longer a few times a day for exercise and attention. Ideally, your sitter will be there as much, if not more, than you are normally home so your dog doesn't feel neglected. It might be hard on your Cockapoo to be away from their favorite person, so a good pet sitter is important.

In any case, make sure to properly vet anyone who will be taking care of your dog. There are tons of websites and apps to help you find someone to watch your dog, but personal recommendations will take you much further. If a friend or coworker can trust their dog with someone, chances are that you can, too. Meet with your sitter or kennel and talk about your dog's needs. Have your dog meet their new caretaker before you leave on your trip. When you're on vacation, the last thing you want to worry about is how your dog is doing. With any luck, you'll return from your trip and go home to a happy puppy.

Traveling can be stressful for a dog. There are so many new sights, sounds, and smells that can be overwhelming to a young pup. The best thing you can do for your dog is to slowly prepare them for new experiences. And when you're planning your trip, keep your dog's temperament in mind. If you know your dog will struggle with all the change, find a good caretaker for the duration of your trip. If you decide your Cockapoo can handle the journey, take measures to make sure they're comfortable and happy. Traveling is stressful enough, so don't add any extra stress by bringing along an ill-prepared Cockapoo.

Photo Courtesy of Tracey Thompson

CHAPTER 15
Grooming Your Cockapoo

"Don't be afraid to learn grooming procedures that you can do at home. Keep their bangs short so they stay out of their eyes. Groom them often and start it young so that they are used to it. Get them used to having their paws handled, their nails trimmed, and the sounds of a clipper at a young age so that their first grooming isn't traumatic."

Jamie

Cute Cockapoos

Cockapoos are beautiful dogs with soft, fluffy coats. Cockapoos love to be the center of attention, so you'll want them looking nice. Grooming is also necessary in maintaining your dog's health. Whether you choose to do your dog's grooming on your own or hire a professional, you'll have to spend some time making sure your dog's hygienic needs are met. Sometimes, dogs don't totally enjoy being groomed, especially when it's more fun to roll around in stinky things; but if you start early, grooming will become a normal part of your dog's routine.

Coat Basics

The Cockapoo coat allows for some variation, depending on how your dog was bred. A straight-coated Cockapoo is possible but very uncommon. A curly or wavy coat is the norm with this breed. Perhaps the best thing about the coat is how little it sheds. This is due to the Poodle's curly coat genes. The coat does not grow excessively long, either.

Like with many other dog breeds, regular brushing is necessary to keep your dog's coat shiny and tangle-free. Brushing helps redistribute natural oils throughout the length of the hair and brushes away dead skin. If a Cockapoo's fur gets tangled and matted, you may have to cut the patch of fur to get rid of the problem. A regular pin brush should be enough to do the trick. If your dog has problems with mats, a slicker brush may also help get down to the root of the problem.

Professional Grooming

This breed can get a little shaggy around the face, so you might decide you want to take your dog to a professional groomer for a quick trim. What the groomer does is up to your preference. Some Cockapoo owners like their dog's coat to be long and full. Others like it to be trimmed and neat, especially during the summer. You can keep your dog as fluffy as you like, but pay special attention to the fur around their eyes and mouth. You may find that this fur gets too long and in the way. Long hairs can fall into the eyes, irritating them. Dirt and germs from outside can make their way from their fur into their sensitive eyes, leading to infection. At the very least, the extra fur might be annoying and make it hard for your dog to see. When this happens, take your pooch in for a trim. As far as breeds that need grooming go, the Cockapoo is fairly low-maintenance.

*Photo Courtesy of
Irene Blackhaw*

Bathing

Eventually, your dog will get so dirty that they will require a bath. When this happens, you'll want to have a few things on hand. First, you'll want a good dog shampoo. Choose one specially formulated for dogs. A gentle solution is best, as to not strip too many natural oils from the skin and hair. It's not absolutely necessary, but a detachable shower hose can make your dog's bath so much easier than filling up a tub and rinsing with a cup. If your dog doesn't take to the water, keep a few treats on hand use as positive reinforcement.

Fill the tub with a few inches of warm water. Give your Cockapoo a quick rinse and then work their fur into a lather with the shampoo. Pay special attention to their face to ensure that no soap or water gets into sensitive areas. It's best to use a damp rag on the face and save the scrubbing for the rest of the body. Give your dog a thorough rinse when you're done. Any excess soap will dry out their skin and make their fur brittle and dull. Once finished, towel dry your Cockapoo and give them a treat to remind them that bath time doesn't have to be a bad time.

Photo Courtesy of Jackie Meredith

If your dog fights you during every bath, try to smear a little peanut butter on the back of the bathtub or shower wall. This will keep them busy for a few minutes while you give them a wash. Also, make sure that the water isn't too hot or too cold. Remember, dogs only need a bath once every few months, unless they're particularly dirty. Otherwise, you'll take away the natural oils that protect their skin and coat.

Trimming Nails

Long claws on a dog are not ideal. Not only do they click and clack on the floor, but they scratch people and furniture. And if toenails grow too long, they can cause foot pain. Nail trimming is something that can be done at home. However, dogs don't always sit patiently and wait for you to cut their nails. Before you even begin to cut nails, practice touching your dog's paws. If they tolerate you touching their paws and nails, give them a treat. This will create a positive association between touching paws and rewards.

When it comes time to trim the nails, clip the nails with tiny snips instead of taking off big chunks. Some dog nail clippers have guards on them so that you don't take too much off. If you cut too much, you might nick the blood supply, or quick. This can be extremely painful and will make your dog hesitant to let you clip them again. If your Cockapoo is too squirmy, this is a service that a groomer can help with. They have lots of experience with a variety of dogs and can get the job done quickly.

Brushing Teeth

Brushing your dog's teeth is about more than keeping them shiny. It also reduces doggy breath and removes harmful plaque from teeth. The condition of a dog's teeth makes a big difference in their overall health. When the teeth begin to decay, it makes it painful for your dog to eat. The bacteria from the decay can wreak havoc on your dog's overall well-being. Bad teeth have been linked to heart disease and can even take years off of an otherwise healthy dog's life.

It may seem like a lot of work but brushing a dog's teeth is not so hard. Before you begin, practice touching your dog's mouth to get them used to the strange feeling. Gently pull their lips back and poke at their teeth. This is also good practice for visiting the vet.

When they're comfortable with you poking around their mouth, it's time to brush! Use a toothbrush and toothpaste made for dogs. Dogs can't spit out toothpaste, so they need a special formula just for them. These kinds of toothpaste come in a variety of dog-friendly flavors. You can decide which type of brush to use, depending on the size of your dog's mouth and your comfort. There are traditional-handled toothbrushes in a variety of sizes or rubber-bristled brushes that slip on over your finger.

When brushing, focus on the outsides of the back teeth. When your dog eats crunchy foods, the kibble scrapes plaque away from the inside parts of the mouth. The outsides tend to collect more of that nasty build-up that leads to disease. Gently brush their teeth, taking care not to injure the gums with rigorous brushing.

The more you brush, the better your dog's teeth will be in the long run. Some owners are great about brushing every night before bed, while others get around to it once a week. Prevention is key when it comes to your dog's teeth. If you can keep your pup's pearly whites clean, then they'll be less likely to need professional cleaning in the future.

Cleaning Ears

Photo Courtesy of
Nataliya Ratosh

Cockapoos have floppy ears that can become fected much more easily than in other breeds. Moisture and bacteria get trapped inside and become a breeding ground for nasty infections. When left untreated, this can cause a lot of pain and potential hearing loss in your dog. For this reason, Cockapoo owners need to pay special attention to their dog's ears.

First, take special care to keep water out of your dog's ears. In the bath, don't rinse their face with the shower hose. You might even want to place cotton balls in the opening of the ear to prevent water from going in. If your dog gets water in their ears when they slurp from their water dish, consider buying a platform to elevate their bowl to keep their head up and their ears away from the splashing water.

If you notice that there's a lot of waxy buildup in your dog's ears and they're scratching and shaking their head a lot, it might be a good time to clean their ears. Pet stores sell ear cleaning solution that's safe for your dog. To use it, squirt the solution directly into the ear. Then, massage the outside of the ear, working the solution down into the ear canal. This liquid will work to break up the wax in the ear. Let your dog shake the extra moisture out and you're good to go! If there's a lot of wax on the ear flap, you may use a moistened cotton ball to gently wipe the residue away. Never use Q-tips or any other small instrument to clean deep inside the ear, as this can damage your dog's delicate inner ear.

Of course, if your dog appears to be itchy or in pain after cleaning, see a vet. They can diagnose infection and prescribe medication to help with your Cockapoo's floppy ears. They will also clean their ears if this is too big of a task for you. Many dogs dislike the sensation of something cold and wet squirted in their ear. Sometimes, it's best to leave the important tasks to the professionals!

Home Grooming vs. Professional Grooming

Photo Courtesy of Kerry Lyon

While it's not absolutely necessary to pay another person to perform these tasks, sometimes it's worth it. If you have a squirmy dog, you risk injuring your pooch with sharp objects like scissors and nail clippers. Professional groomers have a lot of experience and can handle anything that comes their way. They also have an eye for how certain breeds are meant to be trimmed, so they can make your dog look neat and tidy if you're not exactly sure what kind of cut to give.

On the other hand, grooming can be expensive, and it may be hard to find the time to take your dog in for an appointment if you just need to trim a few long nails. Keep grooming equipment on hand in case you ever need it. But if you truly feel uncomfortable doing these tasks, leave it to the groomer. It's not worth injuring or traumatizing your dog if you're not able to do something yourself.

There is much more to dog grooming than just looking pretty. Though your dog loves to eat and roll in all sorts of gross things, cleanliness is very important to their health. Trimmed nails, clean ears, and brushed teeth can improve your dog's quality of life, and maybe even their overall life expectancy. It takes some time and effort, but it's absolutely worth it when your dog looks and feels good.

CHAPTER 16
Nutrition and Healthcare

"I feed my dogs a grain free diet, usually chicken based. Occasionally the fat from a base like duck will upset their gastrointestinal system. Keep it simple. Do not feed a kibble that is devoid of meat (like a pea or lentil based kibble). Dogs are innately carnivores."

Jeanne Davis
Windhorse Offering

There's nothing more important than your dog's health. Unfortunately, our dogs aren't on this earth for long, so every owner wants to make sure they get as many years with their furry friend as possible. And the quality of those years matters, too. Luckily, there are a few things you can do to keep your dog's health top-notch. Along with good hygiene, good nutrition and regular checkups will go a long way to keep your dog happy and healthy.

*Photo Courtesy of
Lee Carpenter*

Importance of a Good Diet

Just like with humans, what you feed your dog matters. If you feed your dog nutritious food, they'll have lots of energy and their body will work efficiently. If they eat junk, their bodies will not get the important things they need. Extra fat will accumulate around organs, causing them to work harder to function.

Because there is a lot of variation in Cockapoo sizes, the food you give your dog may depend on their size. Large breed formulas are for medium- to large-sized dogs, while small breed foods are suited for the mini and yoy sized breeds. Different dogs need slightly different nutrients.

A big dog can stand to have more carbohydrates in their diet because they burn more energy. Smaller dogs tend to need foods higher in protein. Any sized dog should be eating foods with good sources of proteins and carbohydrates. When it comes to protein, multiple meat sources can provide a better range of amino and fatty acids. When it comes to carbohydrates, complex carbs are good at keeping your dog energized and full for longer. Ingredients like oatmeal, brown rice, and barley will keep your dog's stomach from growling between meals.

Also, don't be afraid of fats in your dog's diet. Fats and oils are what keeps your dog's skin moisturized and their coat smooth. Look for foods that have omega fatty acids, like from fish oil. These nutrients are great for the skin and also promote healthy brain activity.

We all know that fruits and vegetables are good for people, but many don't consider all of the vitamins and minerals dogs need in their food. There should be a wide variety of vitamins and minerals at appropriate levels for your Cockapoo's size. Virtually all foods will contain some sort of multivitamin mix, but some contain the actual produce it comes from. Produce contains antioxidants that fight the aging process and keep the immune system healthy. These fruits and vegetables also contain fiber, which keeps your dog regular.

When it comes to feeding your dog, use the feeding guide on the bag to figure out how much they need per meal. The guide will tell you how much food a dog needs by weight. So, it's helpful to have an accurate weight for your dog; otherwise, they might get too much or too little food.

Weight issues aren't very common in this breed because they like to get their exercise and are not prone to overeating. However, if your vet notices that your dog is overweight, it's important to address this concern immediately. Too much weight can be hard on their joints and internal organs. The first thing you will want to do is reduce their daily calories and increase their exercise. Find the right balance of food and exercise to keep them at a stable, healthy weight. Remember that treats add to this calorie count. If you don't see results after a few months, consult your vet to make sure that there aren't other underlying health issues at play.

How to Choose Your Dog's Food

Photo Courtesy of Sandra Mcglynn

Once you know what nutrients your Cockapoo needs to be healthy, it's time to choose a food. This can be a daunting task when you go to the pet store because there are countless options for your furry friend. Each brand boasts different qualities and comes in a wide variety of flavors. So, how do you choose?

If you're buying a dog from a breeder, ask your breeder what they use. This will give you a good idea of the quality of food a Cockapoo enthusiast swears by, and also tell you what your new puppy is used to. Sometimes, dogs can be picky when it comes to flavors. If you don't know what kind of food gets your dog's mouth watering, many stores will offer free samples of kibble to try.

You'll also notice that food comes in wet and dry varieties. The wet foods contain moisture, which makes the food more aromatic and appetizing to a dog. However, it sticks to the teeth. It's easy to eat if your dog has mouth issues, but it is not necessary for a healthy dog. Crunchy food, on the other hand, scrapes the plaque off of teeth every time your dog eats. For this reason, it's best for dogs to eat dry food, as to limit the amount of plaque that develops on your dog's teeth.

Another thing you'll notice is that there's a wide variety of prices in dog food. Cheap dog foods can keep their prices down by using lower quality ingredients. Expensive dog foods often use ingredients that are closer to what people might eat, yet they're not technically human-grade foods. Also, a high price may signal to dog owners that it's a superior product, which may not always be the case. When in doubt, start by examining food labels in the middle of the price range. If the nutrient levels and ingredients look good to you, then it's probably a good dog food.

Homemade Food

Some dog owners make their own dog foods instead of buying commercial brands. While this is unconventional, it's sometimes beneficial for dogs. Occasionally, dogs will have food allergies and intolerances to certain ingredients, making it hard to find a food for their pup. Other times, owners don't like the idea of their dog eating anything lower quality than what they would feed their human family. In any case, making homemade dog food should be done under the supervision of a veterinarian or pet nutritionist to ensure that a dog is not missing any vital nutrients. These experts can recommend recipes and calculate caloric needs. There are tons of websites out there with owner-created recipes for inspiration, but be cautious in who you trust.

People Food

Whether you give your dog people food or prohibit it is controversial amongst dog owners. It's no surprise that dogs love to eat table scraps and any other tasty treat they can get their paws on, but it's not necessarily good for their bodies. When it comes to people food, it's best to err on the side of caution. First of all, you don't want to make your dog sick because the food contained something toxic to dogs. Onions, grapes, avocados, and chocolate are just a few things that humans can eat that make dogs very ill. Some foods, like dairy products, are not necessarily toxic, but your dog may not be able to digest them well, leading to tummy aches and diarrhea. Second, if your dog is eating a balanced diet with their dog food, adding high-calorie globs of fat from your steak trimmings is going to pack on the pounds over time. Finally, if you teach your dog that they can have the occasional scrap from your dinner table, they're going to sit under the table and beg every time you eat. This will become extremely annoying and it's hard to break that habit once it begins.

On the other hand, some owners like to use people food as training treats because they can be nutritious and can be a special treat when used sparingly. Some dogs go crazy for leafy greens, berries, and cooked pumpkin. These are great for dogs because they are low calorie and packed with nutrients. As long as you use these as special treats, it's fine to feed these to your dog on special occasions.

Checkups and Preventative Healthcare

When it comes to the health of your dog, it's best to prevent any issues before they cause harm. One way to do this is to take your dog to the vet for an annual checkup. During this time, they'll ask you if you've noticed any changes in your dog's health or ask if you have any concerns. Even if your concerns turn out to be nothing, it's still a good time to ask any questions you might have.

Your vet will do a quick, but thorough examination of your dog. They'll check the eyes, ears, and mouth for any abnormalities. They'll listen to your dog's heart, lungs, and belly to make sure everything sounds normal. Your dog will have their temperature taken to check for any infection. Finally, the vet will run their hands along your dog to make sure everything is fine with their legs, back, and belly.

The reason it's so important to go every year is that a vet can quickly diagnose an issue you might not even notice. And if you go regularly, they can track changes from year to year, pinpointing issues to keep an eye on. If you only go to the vet when your dog is sick, there's no benchmark when your dog is in healthy state to compare to.

Photo Courtesy of Linda Jones

Fleas, Ticks, and Worms

Part of preventative care is taking precautions to keep parasites off your dog. Dogs are like magnets for these awful creatures because dogs eat things they shouldn't and wander around areas with lots of vegetation. And once the parasites latch on, it may be hard to tell that your dog has an infestation.

Intestinal worms are fairly common in puppies. If you notice your dog's eating habits have changed, their bowel movements are irregular, or they're lethargic or vomiting, it's a good idea to have a vet check them out. A stool sample can quickly reveal if there are any worms in their gut and medicine can be prescribed to take care of the issue. Heartworms are another parasite that travels through the bloodstream. Infected mosquitoes bite your dog, which releases the heartworm into the bloodstream, eventually making its way to the heart. This parasite can be deadly if not treated immediately. Luckily, there's a monthly preventative medicine that can keep your dog protected against heartworm. After a quick blood test, your vet will prescribe a medication to give to your dog monthly. As long as you give this medicine to your dog on a regular basis, you won't have to worry about heartworm.

Fleas and ticks are other nuisances that can easily latch onto your dog. These creatures suck the blood from your dog and can possibly pass on dangerous diseases. Plus, fleas cause extreme itchiness and are hard to kill once an infestation starts. To prevent your dog from bringing these pests home, choose a preventative that works best for your pup. Topical preventatives can be applied to your dog's coat once a month, or there are oral preventatives that cause fleas and ticks to die when they bite your dog. If fleas and ticks cannot survive on your pooch, then there's less of a chance of these pests reproducing and causing your dog harm.

Vaccinations

Vaccinations are another big part of preventative care and are even required by law. There are a handful of contagious diseases that veterinarians can vaccinate against, starting when your dog is a puppy. At many places, your dog must be up to date on their recommended vaccinations in order to take training classes or go to dog parks. The rabies vaccine is required to license your dog because an unvaccinated dog can become a public health risk.

While vaccinations have become a hot topic in recent years, there is no reason not to vaccinate your dog. By keeping your dog free of contagious diseases, you're doing your part in eliminating terrible viruses that kill lots of dogs. You're not only protecting your dog, but also other dogs who might not be up to date on their vaccines. When you get your puppy's first round of shots, your vet will put your dog on a vaccination schedule. The clinic will then notify you every time your dog needs to get booster shots to maintain their immunity.

Genetic Illnesses

"Cockapoos can carry genetic health concerns found in the Cocker Spaniel or Poodle breeds. It's imperative to ask about any testing before buying a Cockapoo. Cocker Spaniels are known for cardiac and eye diseases. Poodles give the longevity genes, but should be tested for hip dysphasia and deformity in elbows. Many breeders use OFA testing or Paw Print Genetics to verify their health."

Luann Woodard
Cockapoo Cottage

Because the Cockapoo is half Cocker Spaniel and half Poodle, common genetic ailments come from both breeds. The good thing about crossbreeds is that they're less likely to suffer from deadly genetic diseases because there's less in-breeding between dogs. Also, if you're buying from a reputable breeder, their practices limit the number of genetic ailments by choosing only healthy dogs to use in breeding. However, there are some ailments that are more common in certain breeds, so it's a good idea to know what to look for.

There are a few conditions of the skeletal system that you'll want to look out for if your dog starts suddenly limping. Luxating patella is a condition in which the kneecap slides around and "catches" in certain circumstances. The simple act of running and jumping can cause the knee to slide out of place, which can be extremely painful. Hip dysplasia is another condition that's generally found in larger breeds where the hip joint doesn't fit in the socket very well, causing pain and issues with mobility. Both conditions need to be treated with surgery if serious enough.

This breed is also more likely to suffer from retinal atrophy and other eye issues. Retinal atrophy can lead to blindness over time. Of course, this is one of those conditions that should be eliminated in the breeding process. However, if you adopt a dog from an unknown origin, you may want to have your dog's eyes tested if they have trouble seeing in the dark. This is a sign that their overall eyesight is deteriorating. Poodle crossbreeds are also at a higher risk for thyroid issues. Talk to your vet if your dog is suddenly lethargic or has patchy fur. They can prescribe medications that can return their hormone levels to normal in no time.

Senior Dog Care

Photo Courtesy of Kelly Cunningham

Cockapoos have a relatively long lifespan compared to other breeds, but one day, they will be considered a senior dog. Senior dogs still love to play and explore, but they will slow down a little, especially compared to the energy levels they had as a puppy.

You may find that your senior dog has joint pain when they try to walk or play. This is often noticeable when they first get up in the morning or try to walk around after a nap. There are a few things you can do to ease this stiffness and pain. For starters, make sure that your dog has a soft and supportive bed to rest on. If they're used to hopping up on the couch, they may have a harder time doing that as they age. There are also joint supplements that you can give your dog that will help repair some of the damage that occurs to leg joints over time. If your dog seems to be in a considerable amount of pain, talk to your vet about anti-inflammatory medication. This may be a good remedy for joint pain.

Your Cockapoo may also gain weight if they're not exercising as much as they used to. Older dogs require fewer calories than their younger counterparts. If your senior dog is gaining weight, consider reducing their daily food intake. If they have trouble eating crunchy kibble due to reduced smell or painful teeth, try mixing dry and wet food together to make it easier to chew. Or pour a little water or broth on top of the crunchy food to soften it up.

You may also have to change your exercise routine. While you may have been able to go on runs before, you will reach a time where that's just too much exertion for your old dog. Exercise is still important, but you may decide that an easy walk will lead to less pain and stiffness in your dog's legs. Continuing to test your dog's mental fitness with puzzles and other games is still important as they get older. It can keep their mind sharp, which will lead to less confusion and agitation.

Most of all, it's important to spend quality time with your Cockapoo. These dogs are companion animals and want to snuggle up to you. You may find that as your Cockapoo ages, he's less interested in playing fetch and more interested in nestling up to you while you read a book. Cherish these moments with your dog because they won't last forever. Also, remember that dogs are considered "senior" around age eight. With proper care, it's entirely possible for your dog to live another decade beyond that.

Eventually, there will come a time where you have to say goodbye. If your dog is in a lot of pain, can no longer use the bathroom on their own, or is suffering from a lot of different age-related ailments, you may decide that euthanasia is the best option. This can be extremely difficult to decide for your pet, but you'll know when your dog's condition will only get worse and their quality of life is suffering. When you're reaching this conclusion, talk to a vet for guidance. An examination can tell you if there's anything they can do for your dog. If not, they will take you through the euthanasia process.

Once you bring your dog home, you'll come to realize that there's nothing more important than ensuring your pup lives the best life he possibly can. The decisions that you make along the way have a lot to do with his health and happiness. Exercise, food, hygiene, and preventative care can extend your dog's lifespan by years and give them lots of quality time with you. Remember that your veterinarian is a great resource, and you should work together to give your dog the healthcare they deserve.

Cockapoos are great companions for a first-time dog owner or an experienced owner of a whole crew! They are adorable, peppy, sweet dogs that love to spend time with their people. Their intelligence makes them easy to train, and their goofiness makes them easy to love. There's a reason that this crossbreed has been popular for so long—they're the total package when it comes to awesome dog breeds!

*Photo Courtesy of
Michelle Clark*

Lightning Source UK Ltd.
Milton Keynes UK
UKHW020617181121
394182UK00001B/26